Seeds for Growth

Financing smallholder farming in southern Africa

Edited by Leslie Nyagah

idasa
AN AFRICAN DEMOCRACY INSTITUTE

First published 2011 by
Idasa
6 Spin Street
Cape Town 8001

© Idasa 2011

ISBN: 978-1-920409-67-8

Editing: Glenda Younge
Proofreading: Alfred le Maitre
Typesetting and design: Red Setter
Cover: Lucid Pictures
Printed and bound by: Mega Digital (Pty), Ltd, Parow Industria 7493

Contents

Acknowledgements

The Public Expenditure and Smallholder Agriculture Project would like to express sincere gratitude to the International Budget Partnership of the Centre on Budget and Policy Priorities for their grant, which has enabled the project and its partners to contribute positively to the issues around the smallholder agricultural landscape in Africa. The grant supported the compilation and production of this volume as an outcome of the first regional conference held by the project on the 9–11 November 2009 in Johannesburg, South Africa.

The Project and its staff would also like to extend a special thank you message to Dr Joe Phaahla, Archbishop Njongonkulu Ndungane, contributing authors, the Idasa Executives and the Economic Governance Programme staff for their enthusiastic support for the production stage of this volume. Thanks are due to the Smallholder Agriculture Project in general as this has proved to be an exciting opportunity to engage with smallholder agriculture issues on the continent whilst at the same breath taking time to learn about the dynamic and varied nature of the opportunities and challenges that confront smallholder farmers.

Equally, the project would like to thank Dr Peter Jacobs of the Human Sciences Research Council (HSRC) for his rigorous external review of all of the volume chapters. His knowledge of the southern African agricultural landscape and agrarian reform processes helped to make this volume more insightful and appealing to all audiences interested in the subject, both within and outside of the region.

The authors write in their personal capacities and their views do not represent nor reflect those of Idasa nor any of their sponsoring bodies.

Acronyms and abbreviations

ACTESA	Alliance for Commodity Trade in Eastern and Southern Africa
ADMARC	Agricultural Development and Marketing Corporation
ADB	African Development Bank
agGDP	Agricultural Gross Domestic Product
AGRF	African Green Revolution Forum
AMSDP	Agricultural Marketing Systems Development Programme (Tanzania)
ANC	African National Congress
ANSAF	Agricultural Non-State Actors Forum
ARC	Agricultural Research Council
ASDP	Agriculture Sector Development Programme (Tanzania)
ASDS	Agriculture Sector Development Strategy
AU	African Union
CAADP	Comprehensive Africa Agriculture Development Programme (NEPAD)
CAG	Controller and Auditor General
CAP	COMESA's Agricultural Policy
CASP	Comprehensive Agricultural Support Programme
CBG	Capacity Building Grant
CBOs	Community Based Organisations
CDO	Community and Development Officer
CISANET	Civil Society Agricultural Network (Malawi)
COMESA	Common Market for Eastern and Southern Africa
CRDP	Comprehensive Rural Development Programme
CSOs	Civil society organisations
CRDP	Comprehensive rural development programme
DADG	District Agriculture Development Grant
DADP	District Agriculture Development Plan
DALDO	District Agriculture and Livestock Development Officer
DC	District Council
DFID	Department for International Development (UK)
DIDF	District Irrigation Development Fund
DOA	Department of Agriculture
DRC	Democratic Republic of Congo
EAFF	East African Farmers Federation
EAC	East African Community
EACSOF	East African Civil Society Forum
EBG	Extension Block Grant
ECOSOCC	Economic, Social and Cultural Council
EPA	Economic Partnership Agreement
ESA	Eastern and Southern Africa
EPA	Economic partnership agreement
EAFF	East African Farmers Federation
ESAFF	Eastern and Southern Africa Small Scale Farmers' Forum
FANR	Food Agricultural and Natural Resources

FAO	Food and Agriculture Organisation of the United Nations
FTA	Free Trade Area
FO	Farmers' organisation
GDP	Gross Domestic Product
GoM	Government of Malawi
GRP	Gross Regional Product
HBS	Household Budget Survey
IDA	International Development Association (World Bank)
IFAD	International Fund for Agricultural Development
IFPRI	International Food Policy Research Institute
IMF	International Monetary Fund
IPFs	Indicative Planning Figures
LGAs	Local Government Authorities
LGRP	Local Government Reform Programmes (Tanzania)
LRAD	Land Redistribution for Agricultural Development
M&E	Monitoring and Evaluation
MAFISA	Micro Agricultural Financial Institution of South Africa
MAFSC	Ministry of Agriculture, Food Security and Cooperatives (Tanzania)
MDAs	Ministries and Development Agencies
MDGs	Millennium Development Goals
MEC	Member of the Executive Council
MGDS	Malawi Growth and Development Strategy
MTEF	Medium Term Expenditure Framework
MoFEA	Ministry of Finance and Economic Affairs
MoU	Memorandum of Understanding
MKUKUTA	Mkakati wa Kukuza na Kuondoa Umasikini Tanzania
MoAFS	Ministry of Agriculture and Food Security (Malawi)
Mt/Ha	Metric tons per hectare
MVIWATA	Farmers' Umbrella Organisation (Muungano wa Vikundi vya Wakulima Tanzania)
M&E	Monitoring and Evaluation
NASFAM	National Smallholder Farmers' Association (Malawi)
NDA	National Department of Agriculture (South Africa)
NEPAD	New Partnership for Africa's Development
NGOs	Non-governmental organisations
NIDF	National Irrigation Development Fund
NSAs	Non-state actors
NSGRP	National Strategy for Growth and Reduction of Poverty (MKUKUTA – Tanzania)
O&OD	Opportunities and Obstacles for Development
ODA	Overseas Development Aid
OR	Tambo – Oliver Reginald Tambo
PAFFO	Pan African Farmers' Forum
PER	Public Expenditure Review
PLAS	Proactive Land Acquisition Strategy
PMO-RALG	Prime Minister's Office – Regional Administration and Local Government

PROPAC	Sub-Regional Platform of Farmers Organisations in Central Africa
PRS	Poverty Reduction Strategy
PTA	Preferential Trade Agreement/Area
R&D	Research and development
RAP	Regional Agricultural Policy
REC	Regional Economic Community
RFSP	Rural Financial Services Programme
RISDP	Regional Indicative Strategy Development Plan (SADC)
ROPPA	Network of Farmers and Agricultural Producers Organisations of West Africa
SA	South Africa
SACAU	Southern African Confederation of Agricultural Unions
SADC	Southern African Development Community
SAPs	Structural Adjustment Programmes
SLAG	Settlement/Land Acquisition Grant
SSA	Sub-Saharan Africa
TAMISEMI	Prime Minister's Officer Regional Administration and Local Government
TDV 2025	Tanzania Development Vision 2025
TSh	Tanzanian shilling
UMAGRI	Maghrebian Farmers Union
URT	United Republic of Tanzania
UN	United Nations
URT	United Republic of Tanzania
US$	United States Dollar
VADP	Village Agriculture Development Plans
VAT	Value Added Tax
WDR	World Development Report
WGI	Worldwide Governance Indicators
WSSD	World Summit on Sustainable Development
WTO	World Trade Organisation
ZNFU	Zambian National Farmers Union

Contributors

PETER JACOBS

Peter Jacobs is Chief Research Specialist in the Economic Performance and Development Research Unit at the Human Sciences Research Council (HSRC). He holds a PhD in Economics and specialises in food security, agricultural and rural development in South Africa and other developing countries. He lectured in the Department of Economics at the University of the Western Cape until 2009, and has recently completed a multi-year National Research Foundation/Research Council of Norway research project on globalisation and the rural poor.

RUSSELL WILDEMAN

Russell Wildeman is Programme Manager of the Economic Governance Project (Idasa) and Project Director of the Affiliated Network of Social Accountability in Africa (ANSA-Africa). He holds a Master's cum laude in Political Management from the University of Stellenbosch and his fields are political behaviour and research methodologies. He joined Idasa in 2000 as an educational researcher, focusing on education finance issues and the implementation of key sectoral policies targeted at the poor. He continues to be active in the education sector in South Africa and is currently involved in high-level discussions about the restructuring of the South African public schooling system. His research interests in education include the contentious notion of effective schools and the search for policy solutions to bring about positive change in disadvantaged schools.

MANYEWU MUTAMBA

Manyewu Mutamba has researched various aspects of agriculture, rural livelihoods, poverty analysis and community-based natural resource management for the past 12 years. He has been involved in conceptualising and implementing research and development projects, developing intervention strategies, and monitoring and evaluation. He analyses qualitative and quantitative data using a number of methods (including statistical packages such as STATA and SPSS) and writes up research outputs for various target audiences. He holds a MSc in Agricultural Economics from the University of Zimbabwe.

Chapter 1
LOVEMORE RUGUBE AND CHARLES MACHETHE

Lovemore Rugube is a visiting lecturer at the Postgraduate School of Agriculture and Rural Development, University of Pretoria, and the Department of Agricultural Economics and Extension at the University of Zimbabwe.

Charles Machethe is a professor of Agricultural Economics and Director of the Postgraduate School of Agriculture and Rural Development at the University of

Pretoria. His research has focused on agricultural and rural development issues, including rural finance, agricultural cooperatives, agricultural development policy, socioeconomic aspects of smallholder irrigation, land reform, farm/non-farm linkages and micro-enterprises.

Chapter 2
PRINCE KAPONDAMGAGA AND MPHATSO DAKAMAU

Prince Kapondamgaga has been involved in development issues for over seven years and has worked as Monitoring and Evaluation Manager, Project/Programmes Coordinator/Manager with Concern Universal and World Vision International (Malawi), among others. He is currently the Executive Director for the Farmers Union of Malawi, which is an umbrella body of 33 farmers' organisations in Malawi.

Mphatso Dakamau has experience in project management, impact assessment, research and economics. He has worked as a research assistant at the IITA and is currently working as the Research and Policy Advocacy Coordinator (economic analyst) at the Farmers' Union of Malawi.

Chapter 3
DAMIAN M. GABAGAMBI

Damian Gabagambi graduated with a MSc in Agricultural Economics from Sokoine University of Agriculture (SUA) in Tanzania in 1998. In 2003 he obtained a PhD at the University of Hohenheim in Stuttgart, Germany, then joined Sokoine University of Agriculture as a lecturer in agricultural economics and agribusiness. Currently he is a senior researcher at Research on Poverty Alleviation (REPOA) in Tanzania. He has done extensive research into agriculture in Tanzania, Africa and South-East Asia.

Chapter 4
RUTH HALL AND MICHAEL ALIBER

Ruth Hall is a senior researcher at the Institute for Poverty, Land and Agrarian Studies (PLAAS) at the University of the Western Cape, where she conducts research into the progress and problems of the land reform programme in South Africa. She holds an MA in Development Studies from the University of Oxford, an Honours degree in Political Studies from the University of Cape Town, and is currently registered for a doctorate in Politics at Oxford University. Her major publications are: *Another Countryside? Policy Options for Land and Agrarian Reform in South Africa* (2009) and, co-edited with Lungisile Ntsebeza, *The Land Question in South Africa: The Challenge of Transformation and Redistribution* (2007).

Michael Aliber is a senior researcher at PLAAS, and holds an MA in Public Policy from the University of Michigan (1988) and a PhD in Agricultural and Applied Economics from the University of Wisconsin (2000). He previously held the post of Research Director at the Human Sciences Research Council in Pretoria, where he conducted research into land reform, rural development and poverty reduction.

From 1998 to 2001 he was a technical assistant to the Department of Land Affairs. He has undertaken research and consultancy work related to land policy in Lesotho, Botswana, Malawi, Uganda, Kenya and South Africa.

Chapter 5
Joe Mzinga

Joe Mzinga is Regional Coordinator of the Eastern and Southern Africa Small-Scale Farmers' Forum (ESAFF). He holds an MA in International Relations from Warsaw University and has worked in the civil society sector and media in eastern and southern Africa for over 10 years. Before joining ESAFF he worked for the Foundation for Civil Society, Tanzania's largest grant-providing organisation. Between 2002 and 2004 he worked with the Tanzania Gender Networking Programme (TGNP). From 1999 he was an assistant news editor at the Tanzania Broadcasting Cooperation (TBC) before taking up the position of Campaigning and Advocacy Officer for the PELUM Association based in Lusaka, Zambia.

Chapter 6
Audax Rukonge

Audax Rukonge has a BSc in Agriculture, specialising in agricultural economics, before completing an MA in Development and International Cooperation majoring in social and public policy. Over the last 13 years he has worked, in different capacities with international organisations engaging in local, national and international policy processes in Tanzania and beyond. Audax Rukonge is currently working with Concern Worldwide in Tanzania in the capacity of Governance Programme Manager, addressing issues related to policy coherence, accountability and transparency in agriculture, water and environmental health and land sub-sectors.

Chapter 7
Benito Eliasi, Stéphanie Aubin and Ishmael Sunga

The authors work with the Southern Africa Confederation of Agricultural Unions (SACAU), a regional, membership-based organisation for farmers.

Benito Eliasi has worked extensively with farmers' oganisations at both regional and national levels. Before joining SACAU he worked with the Farmers' Union of Malawi. He is currently the Capacity Development Adviser for Farmers' Organisations.

Stéphanie Aubin is a policy advisor for SACAU. She has vast experience working with various organisations in Africa in the area of rural development. She has worked previously in countries such as Zimbabwe and Ethiopia with local communities.

Ishmael Sunga is Chief Executive Officer for SACAU. He has extensive experience in the operatives of farmers' organisations at regional and national levels. He has been responsible for setting up governance structures for SACAU as well as assisting in strategically positioning the organisation as a regional body.

Chapter 8: Conclusion
LESLIE NYAGAH

Leslie Nyagah's academic background is in food security policy-making and regulation within a national and international rubric. He has lectured, consulted and volunteered in a number of non-governmental and governmental institutions in Kenya and South Africa. He has been appointed the Agriculture Researcher for the Economic Governance Programme, but he also serves as a project manager for the three-year smallholder farming project.

APPENDIX 1
NJONGONKULU NDUNGANE

Archbishop Ndungane is the founder, president and chair of the board of African Monitor, a pan-African not-for-profit body which harnesses the voice of civil society in Africa and monitors and promotes the effective implementation of promises made by the international community, and Africa's own governments, for the continent's development. Archbishop Ndungane is also a recipient of the 2009 Southern Africa Drivers of Change Award in the individual category.

APPENDIX 2
JOE PHAAHLA

Dr Joe Phaahla was appointed Deputy Minister of Rural Development and Land Reform on 11 May 2009. He is currently serving as Deputy Minister of Arts and Culture in the Republic of South Africa.

Foreword

PETER JACOBS

Agriculture in southern Africa depends on resource-poor smallholder farmers who are trapped at woefully low levels of productivity and who struggle to meet their basic needs. The two exceptions to this state of underdeveloped and depressed agriculture are South Africa, which is dominated by capital intensive large-scale farming, and Malawi, which has an exemplary input subsidy programme targeting smallholders. Indeed, cases of sustainable agricultural progress are limited and best practices are not easily transferable across the sub-continent's varied agricultural landscape. Against this backdrop, what kind of agricultural development is appropriate for sustainable betterment in rural and urban living standards? This critical and policy-relevant question might sound old but a new global context is taking shape which calls for a rethink of this challenging question.

The unfolding context opens new prospects and challenges for agricultural development in southern Africa. Judging from recent global events, three compelling sets of contextual factors deserve to be tracked closely. Firstly, food price crises interact with agro-food production which, in turn, exerts immediate and long-term knock-on effects on both rural and urban household food security. Secondly, the great global recession of 2007/08 impacted on agricultural trade and investment flows, which resulted in drastic reductions in the fiscal resources available to support smallholder agricultural development. Thirdly, adverse climatic transitions pose daunting longer-term obstacles for agriculture. These multiple crises, as events of the past decade have demonstrated, are most likely to converge and interact than to occur as isolated accidents.

The papers assembled in this volume were presented at the November 2009 conference on Governance and Smallholder Agriculture in Southern Africa hosted by Idasa and its partners. In each chapter authors reflect on overarching themes that dominate contemporary efforts to boost Africa's agricultural development. It is interesting to note that investment, productivity and growth concerns that confront the region's agricultural sector feature prominently. Reasons for giving priority to these economic imperatives are easy to grasp if viewed against the backdrop of fluctuations in global agro-food input and output markets that bear heavily on Africa's smallholder farmers.

Agriculture in southern Africa did not escape the worldwide surge in food inflation – with the first signs appearing around 2006. In fact, global agro-food commodity markets are in erratic flux which makes it virtually impossible to reliably forecast medium- to long-term trends. Diverse forces have been blamed for sustaining upward pressures on both production and retail prices of agro-foods: higher fertiliser and fuel input prices; speculation in global agricultural commodity markets; middle-class consumption patterns in India and China; using agro-food outputs as bio-fuels feedstock; and collusion among firms across the agro-food value chains.

Since late 2008 the rate of food price hikes seems to have moderated. Some food prices have actually fallen in absolute value, meaning that they are substantially lower than their 2007/08 peaks, whilst others have merely moved from double-digit to fractional price increments. But there are no clear signs that the benefits of lower food inflation will instantaneously trickle down to the food-insecure poor. For the period ahead, the core food basket could remain expensive or unafford-able to economically vulnerable families. Food riots, such as those that erupted in Mozambique's capital, Maputo, as a direct consequence of steep food price inflation, threaten large-scale political turmoil.

Across Africa, recent food price crises triggered various country and regional responses to mitigate the effects of food insecurity. The African Development Bank (ADB), for example, has developed a food crisis response framework to counter immediate and longer-term negative consequences linked to the food price cri-sis. Its longer-term responses, aligned to the Comprehensive Africa Agricultural Development Programme (CAADP), include boosting investment in farm produc-tion infrastructure, particularly water infrastructure. In an effort to cut post-harvest losses, the ADB interventions also focus on upgrading rural roads, better access to markets and storage facilities. A key learning from documented experiences to date suggests that interventions to counter dramatic agro-food price surges must target the entire agricultural value chain, given that more African countries are becoming net food importers and an increasing percentage of rural households are becoming net food purchasers. Agro-food trading regimes and the workings of local output markets are fundamental rather than residual determinants in the modern food security equation.

At the height of the global food price crisis, the spill-over effects from the global economic downturn hit economies in the region that depended on external trade and capital flows. This externally induced recession wiped out several years of posi-tive growth, which had begun to translate into lower rates of poverty and unem-ployment – albeit short of meeting the MDG targets. Moreover, the economic downturn once again exposed Africa's ongoing dependency on a limited range of primary commodity exports and the slow pace of diversification into sectors with higher external economies of scale. Dividends from recent commodity price booms, which ought to have benefited the continent given its comparative advantage in this domain, have not been converted into a resilient development platform.

Recovery in macroeconomic growth is under way, driven by 'stimulus pack-ages' and tighter trade and investment connections with China and India. However, higher living standards always lag behind economic growth. It is unclear how long it might take before sustainable betterment in human wellbeing – poverty, unem-ployment and inequality eradication – sets in. Short- to medium-term anti-crisis interventions include strengthened social safety nets for vulnerable groups, but in the context of sharply reduced fiscal resources, trade-offs are inevitable. Closing the investment gap that has widened as a consequence of the economic downturn has been the key longer-term response. The contraction in official development assistance (ODA) for agriculture is unlikely to reverse, as both Europe and the United States channel resources into domestic ventures to lift their economies to sustainable recovery.

It is too early for any conclusive statements on what these developments imply for existing investment schemes to boost agricultural productivity – especially the seed and fertiliser investment programmes in Malawi and Tanzania. In the meanwhile there has been a surge in land investment by foreign states and powerful multinational firms in strategic areas of southern Africa. Available evidence suggests that the volume of such externally-driven farmland purchases in five countries could be in the order of 2.5 billion ha of land for deals exceeding 1,000 ha. What factors are behind this 'great land grab'? Foreign investors appear to be motivated by food security concerns in their own countries, rapid expansion in bio-fuels production for energy security and lucrative returns from speculation in rising land values. This has the potential to take land out of agro-food production for domestic human needs, but reliable quantitative evidence is lacking to assuage rising fears on this front.

Investment in smallholder agriculture cuts across chapters in the first section of this volume. These chapters dwell extensively on the magnitude of finances allocated to buy farm inputs (such as infrastructure and innovative technologies) yet sidestep a direct focus on investing in farmland as a vital agricultural input. Authors generally observe that smallholder agricultural development is not receiving enough public money, but this is spread unevenly across countries in southern Africa. The benchmark that underpins this conclusion is the Maputo Declaration, which commits countries in the region to allocate 10 per cent of their total national budget to investment in agriculture. It will be increasingly difficult to reach this target as governments try to counter the impacts of the global economic downturn.

A persuasive crowding-in argument exists for the mobilisation of public finance for smallholder agriculture. This implies spill-over effects from state investment in that it acts as a catalyst to leverage private capital inflows into agriculture – especially from non-state financial institutions. Over time, it is expected that public investment in smallholder farming should enable beneficiary farmers to make complementary investments, which could be part of the criteria to assess the efficacy of state-funded agricultural development interventions. In order to examine such second round effects robustly, one requires coherent and reliable longitudinal farm household data but, unfortunately, such information is lacking.

Gazing into the future, investment in agriculture must enable farmers to adapt to and cope in dramatically adverse agro-climatic conditions. Steering resources towards agro-ecologically sustainable farming practices is one way to substantially cut the carbon footprint of fossil-fuel-dependent agriculture. This ought to be part of the criteria to evaluate high-level initiatives that promote an African Green Revolution Forum (AGRF). Drawing largely on funding from the Gates Foundation and chaired by Mr Kofi Annan, former United Nations Secretary-General, the AGRF brings together global diplomats, donors and continental agricultural interests to champion the cause of Africa. Its key initiatives are to promote and sponsor bread-basket project plans and investment blueprints for agricultural growth corridors in Ghana and Tanzania, respectively.

Governance is a cross-cutting theme in the second section of this book. Similar to institutions, this is a multifaceted concept which refers to the rules that define power relations and how associational formations or structures function. It starts from the premise that the quality of administration or management of private and public agencies hinder or help broader socioeconomic development. Widely fashionable conceptual tools, such as the Worldwide Governance Indicators (WGI) developed by the World Bank, now exist to measure the benefits of 'good governance' and support claims that it translates into higher economic growth. The popularity of this contested idea spread progressively as countries began to embrace deregulation, market liberalisation and shrinking active state intervention in the economy. It is integral to the swift transition from the era of liberation from colonial rule to the period of structural adjustment and neoliberalism.

In compliance with the prescriptions of this economic development orthodoxy, African states have withdrawn from agricultural production and markets. The bureaucracy is lauded as efficient if it creates an environment for commercial agricultural interests to maximise returns on investment. In this volume, governance is not restricted to arguments for clean and transparent management of public resources. It defines governance in terms of a bottom-up approach in which smallholder farmers through their associations set agricultural development priorities.

In summary, this volume is a critical review of the status of smallholder agricultural development in southern Africa and highlights a range of options to boost agriculture in a challenging global economic and agro-ecological setting. It is an invaluable synthesis of cutting-edge evidence, analysed from multiple perspectives, for grounded agricultural development policy-making, and will be an essential reference to everyone active in southern Africa's agricultural policy arena. This collection provides a resource for researchers in the region which will help them to identify knowledge gaps for future research.

Peter Jacobs is with the Human Sciences Research Council.

Locating demands for good governance and effective service delivery in a programme context

RUSSELL WILDEMAN

The Economic Governance Programme of Idasa focuses on two cross-sectoral themes, namely, social accountability and public finance. Social accountability focuses on the agency of citizens in their quest for improved governance and effective service delivery, while our public finance work investigates how formal governmental institutions respond to the exigencies of the social and economic needs of citizens. Our work therefore foregrounds both citizen agency and responsive institutions and this approach is based on our conception that both citizens and institutions matter in the quest for good governance and effective service delivery that makes a difference to the lives of ordinary citizens.

Our focus on social accountability does not imply a one-sided focus on the activities and the agendas of civil society. While we champion the importance of civil society work, we believe it is necessary that this work has an immediate and relevant contact point with what democratically elected governments choose to do. Although we do not insist on a perfect reconciliation of the demand-side of our work (civil society and other non-state actors) with the supply-side dimensions of our work (engaging with governments and public institutions), we attempt to facilitate the spaces in which governments and their citizens meet to discuss key social and economic issues. This focus does not only require a slavish commitment to quantitative targets as exemplified in the number of meetings among local stakeholders, but we believe that quality public dialogues are essential to sustain any form of social contract between citizens and their governments. In our approach, we believe that social dialogue and the attempt at constructing a social contract is an ongoing process and that the parameters of this process are best negotiated among local and regional stakeholders. In the Smallholder Farmer and Governance Project, we give expression to this idea through the promotion of active mobilisation of smallholder farmers in order to cultivate a more coherent policy voice in national budgetary and policy debates. While there are undeniable risks to the aggregation of potential in-country smallholder farmer agendas, we judge the formation and activation of such networks as being vital to inserting smallholder farmer concerns into national and regional agricultural debates. This should help to offset the urban bias in elite policy-making, which has consistently denied the importance of agriculture in countering poverty.

Our public finance work focuses on institutions and institutional reform, and targets specific social sectors that have a direct bearing on the fortunes of poor and vulnerable individuals. The institutional dimension highlights the extent to which budgetary institutions have been reformed to enable vibrant contributions from citizens and civil society organisations in the making of national and sectoral budgets. For us, this contribution by civil society and citizens is not only convenient in a procedural sense, but we believe that the clear articulation of the needs of citizens should impact positively on the substantive outcomes. While our work continues to support a systemic and institutional engagement with budgets and the budget process, we believe that complementary sectoral finance work should continue to be pursued. In the Smallholder and Governance Project, we rally behind the Maputo Declaration, which requires that signatories spend at least 10 per cent of the national budget resources on the agriculture sector. Apart from accepting and affirming this generic spending goal, we advocate through our in-country partners for targeted increases that benefit smallholder farmers. This includes the provision of appropriate economic infrastructure, supportive credit markets, effective extension support and technical support to smallholder farmers to increase and diversify their crop yields. Functioning within a programme context means that targeted spending not exclusively destined for the agriculture sector, such as the maintenance and construction of social and economic infrastructure, can be easily articulated as part of our wider concerns with effective fiscal support to the vulnerable and needy in sub-Saharan African societies. There is great value in pursuing a broader sectoral agenda and not to become advocates for any one particular sector when the nature of social and economic development requires an interdependent approach and perspective.

It is for this reason that social accountability and public finance perspectives matter, because we believe that communities, together with their respective governments, need to make appropriate policy choices that benefit all relevant social and economic sectors. This necessitates the establishment of a social compact or contract, and in this regard our work deviates from the traditional sectoral advocacy strategies pursued in civil society. In our view, an exclusive sectoral approach defers policy and budgetary decision-making needlessly to governments, thus foregoing a golden opportunity to influence such agendas in a direct and engaged manner. Although the focus of this book is on the promotion of small-scale agriculture, we would like to continue to affirm the importance of a cross-sectoral approach and the use of both social accountability and public finance tools to keep the smallholder farmer agenda alive. This unified approach is the hallmark of what we are trying to do as a programme and it is in this spirit that we offer in this engaging book, a series of policy, budgetary and governance perspectives on the efforts of smallholder farmers.

Russell Wildeman is Programme Manager of the Economic Governance Project (Idasa) and Project Director of the Affiliated Network of Social Accountability in Africa (ANSA-Africa).

Introduction: Public investment and smallholder agricultural transformation in Africa

Manyewu Mutamba

Unlocking the potential of smallholder agriculture through sustained public investment by governments could transform the lives of large numbers of poor households in rural communities across Africa.

Africa's failure to transform its agricultural sector as rapidly as the rest of the developing world has left a legacy of poverty and hunger. A huge increase in the number of rural people living in absolute poverty underscores the need for urgent attention to measures that could promote agricultural growth. The dominance of smallholder agriculture on the continent means that short- and medium-term agricultural growth and poverty reduction prospects will be closely linked with successful transformation of this sector. Central to the transformation of smallholder agriculture is the need to urgently reverse the current trend of gross undercapitalisation by increasing governments' budgetary resources to the sector. Increased government expenditure should be accompanied by better prioritisation within the sector to target programmes and investments that best address the sector's poor performance in ways that improve the livelihood of large numbers of rural households. Public spending is one of the most direct and effective instruments that governments can use to promote agricultural growth and poverty reduction. Despite this opportunity, lack of commitment to support adequate investment in agriculture has persisted. Even the numerous continent-wide and regional protocols by African governments asserting their commitment to change the status quo has only resulted in limited improvements.

The role and performance of smallholder agriculture in Africa

The population of the sub-Saharan Africa region is projected to grow from some 770 million in 2005 to about 2 billion by 2050. Although rapid rural-urban migration is expected to reduce the proportion of people living in rural areas from the current 70 per cent to around 30 per cent in 2050, the absolute number of rural dwellers will continue to grow.[1] Producing enough food for a growing population, while at the same time combating poverty and hunger are the main challenges facing African agriculture in the coming decades. The risks that come with climate change make this task even more daunting.

African agriculture remains largely subsistence-oriented, dominated by smallholders and pastoralists. There are around 33 million family farm holdings of less

---

1 See FAO, 2008. *State of Food and Agriculture: World Food and Agriculture in Review.* Rome, Italy: FAO.

than two hectares, representing 80 per cent of all farms in sub-Saharan Africa.[2] Although its contribution to GDP is declining, agriculture remains an important economic sector in Africa, contributing around 25 per cent of GDP compared with the world averages of less than 7 per cent.[3] The sector provides jobs for 70 per cent of the labour force as well as a livelihood for over 65 per cent of the population. Given its strong linkages with other sectors, agriculture is a major source of raw materials as well as a market for finished products.

In the SADC region, agriculture accounts for more than 20 per cent of GDP in six countries – DRC, Madagascar, Malawi, Mozambique, Tanzania and Zambia (Table 1a). Ranking amongst the poorest in Southern Africa, these six countries produce 76 per cent of the region's agricultural GDP. The average share of agriculture in regional GDP, excluding South Africa, is 13.7 per cent (Table 1b). This contribution drops to 12.8 per cent when South Africa is included. Tanzania now has the region's largest agricultural sector, having overtaken South Africa between 2000 and 2008. Although the agricultural sector in South Africa is small relative to other sectors (under 4 per cent of GDP), it is still larger than the rest of SADC countries (excluding Tanzania) put together.

Given the urgency to transform African agriculture, the sluggish performance of the sector over the past few decades is disconcerting. Growth rates in this sector across sub-Saharan Africa have only increased modestly from about 2.4 per cent a year between 1980 and 1989, to 2.7 per cent between 1990 and 1999, and 3.3 per cent per year since 2000.[4] Only a handful of countries – Ethiopia, Mali, Mozambique, Nigeria, Senegal and the Gambia – have surpassed the Comprehensive Africa Agriculture Development Programme (CAADP) threshold of 6 per cent in agricultural growth in recent years.[5] Although crop output has been increasing, this is largely driven by expansion of cultivated land rather than productivity improvements. For instance, between 1990 and 2006 the area under cultivation increased by more than 10 per cent annually, while cereal yields over the same period were largely stagnant, averaging around 1.2 tonnes per hectare in the region, compared to 3 tonnes per hectare in the developing world as a whole.[6]

Similarly, the agricultural sector in the SADC region performed poorly in recent years, with few exceptions – Angola, Malawi, Mozambique and Namibia (Table 2). It has to be noted that Angola and Mozambique have started from a very low base following many years of conflict and limited agricultural activity. Malawi has been implementing an extensive agricultural subsidy programme which now seems to be producing remarkable results. During much of this period, agriculture in Botswana, Mauritius, South Africa and Zimbabwe registered negative growth. The CAADP target of a 6 per cent growth rate in agricultural GDP has only been achieved by

---

2 Ibid.
3 See UNECA, 2009. *Economic Report on Africa 2009*. Addis Ababa, Ethiopia: UNECA.
4 Ibid.
5 See FAO, 2010. Food and Agriculture Statistics, Rome. http://www.fostat.fao.org/
6 UNECA, op cit.

Table 1a: Agriculture GDP in SADC countries
Agric GDP (constant 2000 US$ million)

	1990	2000	2006
Angola	685.9	473.1	1,642.6
Botswana	154.7	139.0	133.8
Congo DR	2,011.1	2,407.3	2,204.3
Lesotho	121.7	125.7	118.0
Madagascar	859.8	1,014.8	1,158.4
Malawi	301.6	590.5	658.3
Mauritius	273.8	230.0	274.5
Mozambique	697.6	999.8	1,408.7
Namibia	222.6	311.9	355.8
South Africa	3,691.6	3,777.2	3,590.0
Swaziland	143.9	155.5	149.9
Tanzania	2,766.7	3,649.8	5,016.9
Zambia	471.5	633.8	667.0
Zimbabwe	857.9	1,137.5	710.7
SADC including SA	13,260.3	15,715.9	18,088.7
SADC excluding SA	9,568.7	11,763.7	14498.7

Source: FAOSTAT, accessed 2010

Table 1b: Agriculture share of GDP in SADC countries
Agriculture value added (% of GDP)

	1990	2000	2006
Angola	17.9	5.7	9.6
Botswana	4.9	2.4	2.0
Congo DR	31.0	50.0	45.7
Lesotho	23.8	17.9	17.2
Madagascar	28.6	29.2	27.5
Malawi	45	39.5	35.5
Mauritius	13.1	5.9	5.6
Mozambique	37.1	26.1	21.7
Namibia	11.7	11.0	11.3
South Africa	4.6	3.3	2.5
Swaziland	13.3	15.5	10.9
Tanzania	46.0	45.0	45.3
Zambia	20.6	22.3	16.1
Zimbabwe	16.5	18.5	21.9
SADC including SA	8.3	8.2	7.3
SADC excluding SA	19.4	20.0	18.2

Data source: FOASTAT, accessed 2010

Angola, Malawi, Mozambique and Namibia (Table 2). To reach this target, SADC as a whole needs to raise growth rates by at least 2 per cent. Some countries (DRC, Lesotho, Madagascar, Swaziland and Zimbabwe) need increases of more than 3 per cent to reach this target.

Underlying the poor performance of the agricultural sector in the SADC region is a stagnation or decline in productivity for a number of key subsectors. Since 2000 cereal yields have been on the decline in the region, averaging between 2.3 and 3 mt/ha (Table 3). The only countries to register any significant cereal yield increases between 1999 and 2007 are Mauritius and South Africa, and Malawi since 2007.[7] The region needs to increase its cereal yield by over 400 kg/ha to meet the SADC Regional Indicative Strategic Development Plan (RISDP) target of 2000 kg/ha. Although the yields of roots and tubers increased during the late 1990s (reaching 13.4 mt/ha compared to the average of 8 mt/ha in the rest of Africa), they have since stagnated at the 2000 levels. Malawi did, however, manage to double yields for roots and tubers between 1999 and 2007.[8] Fertiliser use, a strong driver of crop productivity growth, averaged about 44 kg/ha in the SADC region between 1990 and 2005. The RISDP target to increase fertiliser consumption to 65 kg/ha has been achieved only by Mauritius and South Africa.

With the exception of Mauritius, Malawi, Mozambique and South Africa, the region's livestock sector has contracted in recent years. Between 2000 and 2007, Namibia, Lesotho and Swaziland suffered large declines. Livestock production in the SADC region as a whole grew by barely 2 per cent over this period.[9] The RISDP target to increase livestock production by at least 4 per cent annually has only been achieved by Mauritius. The region as a whole must increase production by over 2 per cent, with DRC requiring an increase of over 4 per cent, and Namibia and Swaziland each requiring increases of over 9 per cent.[10]

The poor performance of the agricultural sector has had dire consequences for sub-Saharan Africa. The region has seen a huge increase in the number of people living in absolute poverty – from 214 million in 1981 to 391 million in 2005, with only a small decrease in percentage terms over the same period, from 54 to 51 per cent.[11] Whereas many developing regions, especially in Asia and the Pacific, are on track to meet the first Millennium Development Goal (MDG) of halving poverty by 2015, sub-Saharan Africa is expected to have more poor people in 2015 than it did in 1990.[12]

With six out of 10 people in the SADC region living in rural areas, the poor performance of the agricultural sector in the region has seriously undermined the livelihood of over 150 million people.[13] The region-wide average per capita GDP

---

7 FAO, 2010, op cit.
8 Ibid.
9 FAO, 2010, op cit.
10 Chilonda *et al.*, 2008, op cit.
11 UNECA, 2009, op cit.
12 FAO, 2010, op cit.
13 See World Bank, 2009. *World Development Report 2009.* Washington, DC: World Bank.

Table 2: Annual agricultural growth rates in SADC countries, 1990–2006
Average annual growth in agric GDP (%)

	1990–2000	2000–2003	2003–2006	2005–2006
Angola	–2.8	14.0	28.9	60.5
Botswana	–1.1	1.8	–3.0	3.0
Congo DR	0.6	–0.8	2.0	2.5
Lesotho	1.3	–5.2	0	1.8
Madagascar	1.8	1.3	2.8	2.2
Malawi	7.5	0.8	1.2	10.9
Mauritius	–1.7	5.4	0.6	–4.8
Mozambique	2.4	9.8	6.3	9.0
Namibia	4.3	0.9	0.9	0.6
South Africa	0.7	0.3	-3.5	–13.1
Swaziland	0.4	-1.8	1.9	2.2
Tanzania	3.2	4.8	4.9	3.8
Zambia	3.2	0.2	1.0	–0.6
Zimbabwe	3.2	–9.7	–6.3	–5.8
SADC including SA	1.7	1.8	2.9	2.7
SADC excluding SA	2.1	2.3	4.8	7.5

Source: FAOSTAT, accessed 2010

Table 3: Yields (tonnes/ha) of roots & tubers and cereals in SADC region, 2000–2006

	2000	2001	2002	2003	2004	2005	2006
Roots & tubers	10.2	10.5	10.5	10.0	10.3	10.5	10.7
Cereals	1.7	1.6	1.6	1.5	1.5	1.7	1.6

Source: FAOSTAT, accessed 2010

between 2000 and 2008 was about US$1,790, but an overwhelming majority of countries averaged US$500 or less.[14] With the exception of South Africa, countries whose agricultural sectors performed poorly between 2000 and 2008 also registered low per capita GDP levels. Countries with relatively large agricultural sectors and large rural populations (DRC, Malawi, Mozambique, Madagascar, Tanzania, Zambia, Lesotho and Zimbabwe) recorded especially low per capita GDPs. On the other hand, countries with relatively small agricultural sectors and rural populations (Botswana, Mauritius, Seychelles and Swaziland) fared much better.[15]

Data on money-metric poverty levels in the SADC countries are patchy and inconsistent, but it appears that not much progress has been made. Among the countries where fairly credible data is available, Mozambique appears to have had the greatest success in cutting poverty. Between 1996 and 2002 the national poverty

---

14 Chilonda *et al.*, 2008, op cit.
15 Ibid.

rate fell by about 15 per cent. Also performing well is Malawi, whose national poverty rate fell also by 14 per cent between 1990 and 2007. Lesotho managed a 10 per cent reduction between 1995 and 2003, although the overall level remained at over 50 per cent.[16] Overall, countries have made little progress towards attaining the MDG of halving the proportion of people living in hunger and extreme poverty by 2015. For instance, Malawi's national poverty rate was 54 per cent in 1990 and 51 per cent in 2004. Zambia's national poverty rate increased from 70 per cent in 1990 to 74 per cent in 1993, before declining to 73 per cent in 1998 and 64 per cent in 2006. South Africa's poverty rate fell from 50 per cent in 1993 to 47 per cent in 2004. Madagascar reduced its national poverty rate by 2 per cent between 1997 and 1998, and Tanzania had a 5 per cent reduction between 1991 and 2007. Zimbabwe's poverty rate increased by 9.1 per cent between 1990 and 1995, while Mauritius's national poverty rate also increased by 0.3 per cent between 2002 and 2007.[17]

The food price crisis of 2007/08 highlighted the dramatic implications of a faltering agriculture sector and underscored the need for urgent attention to measures that could turn around the decline in agricultural productivity. Early measures of the impacts of rising food prices on poverty in the region indicate that staple food price increases have a direct correlation with increases in poverty. For example, the rising food prices resulted in 2 and 4.4 per cent increases in poverty in Malawi and Zambia, respectively.[18] The impact in Malawi was relatively lower, perhaps because of the country's recent successful efforts to boost agricultural production, which has made it an important exporter of food to other countries in southern Africa. Other countries are likely to be even more vulnerable. FAO lists four SADC countries among those already facing food crises as a result of high food prices: DRC, Lesotho, Swaziland and Zimbabwe.[19]

Trends in agricultural investment

Foremost amongst the factors that undermine smallholder agriculture in sub-Saharan Africa is the gross undercapitalisation of the sector. Investment in key facets such as research, infrastructure development, mechanisation, irrigation, value chain development and human capital development lags behind that in other developing regions and has actually declined over the past decade. For instance, between 1981 and 2000, public spending on agricultural research and development in the countries of the region grew at only 0.6 per cent per year on average, and actually fell during the 1990s.[20] At the same time, donor support for agricultural research declined from $6 billion in 1980 to $3 billion in 2006 and World Bank

---

16 Ibid.
17 Ibid.
18 See Ivanic, M. Martin, W., 2008. *Implications of Higher Global Food Prices for Poverty in Low-Income Countries.* Policy Research Working Paper WPS 4594. Washington, DC: World Bank.
19 See FAO, 2008. *State of Food and Agriculture: World Food and Agriculture in Review.* Rome, Italy: FAO.
20 UNECA, 2009, op cit.

lending to agriculture in general decreased from $8 billion in 1980 to $2 billion in 2004. The decline in donor funding, which stood at 35 per cent of agricultural research funding in 2000, implies that governments have to rely more on domestic sources. Countries such as Botswana, Burundi, Ethiopia, Gabon, Malawi and the Sudan already fund over 60 per cent of agricultural research from domestic sources. The private sector contributes only 2 per cent of total agricultural research funding in Africa, and its contribution varies across sub-regions and countries, ranging from 1.6 per cent in East Africa to about 4.3 per cent in South Africa.[21]

Historically, agricultural spending in Africa has been very low compared with other developing regions. For instance, African public spending on agriculture between 1980 and 2005 accounted for 5 to 7 per cent of the total national budget, whereas agricultural allocations in Aindenta were between 6 to 15 per cent. As a percentage of agricultural Gross Domestic Product (agGDP), African agricultural spending was only half that of Asia in 2005.[22] Expenditure on agricultural research as a percentage of agGDP is considered adequate at 2 per cent or more.[23] Worldwide expenditure on agricultural research is about 1 per cent of agGDP – over 2.5 per cent in developed countries, 0.6 per cent in developing countries and 0.7 per cent in Africa. Agricultural research expenditure as a ratio of agGDP in southern Africa (2.28 per cent) and South Africa (3.04 per cent) is higher than the global average, but for other sub-regions in Africa the ratio is far less.[24]

In an effort to address this situation, African heads of state adopted the Maputo Declaration on Agriculture and Food Security in 2003, committing their countries to allocate at least 10 per cent of national budgetary resources to the agricultural sector. This level of investment in agriculture was deemed necessary to support an annual growth rate of 6 per cent set by the New Partnership for Africa's Development (NEPAD) through its Comprehensive Africa Agriculture Development Program (CAADP) on food security and poverty reduction. So far, progress towards this goal has been disappointing. According to a validation workshop organised by NEPAD in December 2008, only 19 per cent of African countries have reached this target.[25] Many countries hardly reach 4 per cent of the total national budget and have depended on Overseas Development Assistance (ODA) to fund agriculture. Only a few African countries – Burkina Faso, Ethiopia, Malawi and Mali – have surpassed the 10 per cent threshold of budgetary spending on agriculture in recent years. In fact, nearly half of African countries reduced their spending on the sector during this period.

Most countries in the SADC region have yet to achieve the Maputo Declaration target of allocating 10 per cent of public expenditure to the agricultural sector (Table 4). Only Malawi has consistently exceeded the target in recent years, following

21 World Bank, 2009, op cit.
22 Chilonda *et al.*, 2008, op cit.
23 FAO, 2008, op cit.
24 UNECA, 2009, op cit.
25 Chilonda *et al.*, 2008, op cit.

Table 4: Share of public expenditure on agriculture in SADC countries (2003–2007)

	2003–2004	2004–2005	2005–2006	2006–2007
Angola	-	2.24	6.47	5.29
Botswana	2.8	2.7	3.2	3.3
DRC	0.8	0.7	1.5	1.8
Lesotho	4.8	5.0	4.0	3.5
Madagascar	8.0	7.9	8.0	8.0
Malawi	6.6	12.7	11.0	13.2
Mauritius	2.7	3.4	2.9	2.9
Mozambique	6.2	4.4	3.4	3.9
Namibia	7.3	6.9	8.2	8.0
Swaziland	5.0	6.0	4.7	3.7
Tanzania	5.7	4.7	5.8	5.8
Zambia	1.8	3.2	3.6	4.0
Zimbabwe	9.4	10.0	6.2	6.0
SADC	5.1	5.4	5.3	5.3

Source: FAOSTAT, accessed 2010

a government input subsidy programme. Despite this rather disappointing trend, it is encouraging that between 2003 and 2007, all but four SADC countries (Lesotho, Mozambique, Swaziland and Zimbabwe) increased their share of allocations to agriculture. Prior to 2005, Zimbabwe's share was only slightly below the target, but since then it has fallen sharply as a direct result of political and economic strife.

Deviations from the 10 per cent target vary widely across the region. On average the SADC region needs an increase in public expenditure on agriculture of about 5 per cent to reach the target. Eight countries need increases larger than 5 per cent. Botswana, DRC and Mauritius face the greatest challenges as they need percentage increases of between 7 and 9 per cent. Ongoing political instability in the DRC seems to have taken a toll on the country's focus on the agricultural sector. Despite consistent and significant economic progress in Botswana recently, the agricultural sector has been neglected, perhaps at the expense of the dominant and highly lucrative mining sector. A radical change in policy priorities will be required for these countries to turn around this trend and make meaningful progress towards the CAADP targets.

Background to the book

This book is a product of a conference on Governance and Smallholder Agriculture in the SADC region organised by Idasa and its partners in late 2009. The aim of the conference was to discuss governance and public investment trends and how these are shaping transformation of smallholder agriculture in the region. Specifically, the meeting focused on three sub-themes: (i) priorities for public investment in agriculture; (ii) trends in public expenditure on smallholder agriculture; and (iii) policy processes and stakeholder participation. The conference was structured as paper presentations and discussions around the three sub-themes. Some presented papers were selected for inclusion in this book following a post-conference review of each paper.

Sub-theme 1: Priorities for public investment in agriculture

This sub-theme explored lessons and best practices that are emerging from work done on prioritisation and sequencing of public investments aimed at transforming smallholder agriculture to achieve pro-poor outcomes. In the last couple of years, there has been renewed focus on smallholder agriculture as a potential driver for growth and poverty reduction in sub-Saharan Africa. Governments and development agencies alike have expressed enthusiasm on the potential for smallholder agriculture-led growth and poverty reduction despite a record of failed agricultural investments in Africa. It is now widely acknowledged that agriculture-based investments have the potential to drive broader economic growth, and also provide the best prospects for pro-poor development outcomes, as poverty is most chronic in rural parts of Africa where over 65 per cent of the African population lives. Because of the complexity of most rural livelihood systems, details on the form of investments that should be prioritised, and the sequencing of such investments under different socioeconomic contexts however remain poorly understood. These shortcomings have undermined investment efforts to reduce poverty through transformation of smallholder agriculture.

Specifically the sub-theme explored the following questions:

- To what extent does smallholder agriculture provide realistic opportunities for rural populations to lift themselves out of poverty?
- What are the current trends in investment to support smallholder agriculture and how effective have they been in different African countries?
- What areas of investment in agricultural/rural development offer the best returns and how is this affected by the socioeconomic context?
- What are the most effective approaches to the sequencing of investments to support smallholder agriculture?

Sub-theme 2: Trends in public expenditure and smallholder agriculture

This sub-theme focused on the trends in public expenditure on agriculture and the nature and magnitude of its impact on smallholder agriculture in the region. Despite signing many regional protocols pledging their commitment to increase investment in agriculture many African governments have not taken concrete actions at the scale required to transform the sector and rural livelihoods in general. The lack of effective farmer organisational systems and limited support from civil so-ciety groups have undermined the ability of smallholder farmers to put pressure on governments to keep to their commitments. Specifically the sub-theme was aimed at investigating the following:

- What are the trends in government expenditure on smallholder agriculture and how effective are these in promoting pro-poor economic growth?
- How does government spending on agriculture compare with their stated commitments (for example, the Maputo Declaration), and what advocacy strategies are most effective in holding governments accountable to their commitments?
- How can public expenditure programmes be sufficiently targeted to enable smallholder farmers to capture their full benefits?

Sub-theme 3: Stakeholder participation in agriculture policy

Stakeholder participation is a common practice in contemporary development policy-making. This is crucial in establishing ownership and a demand driven process from a stakeholder perspective. A key constraint is the lack of sufficient and accessible information to enable stakeholders at different levels to engage adequately in open dialogue and negotiation processes on issues that affect their welfare. This issue remains a major challenge for smallholder agricultural policy formulation processes across Africa. Farmer groups remain marginal to processes of public expenditure and priority setting, without a voice to influence political decisions that affect the sector. Often, they are not sufficiently organised or informed enough to engage other more sophisticated stakeholders with concrete alternative proposals that better represent the needs and aspirations of the smallholder farmers. This theme aimed to explore models of stakeholder participation in agricultural policy-making processes and to distils key lessons on making these more effective. Specifically this theme investigates the following questions:

- What are the current models of stakeholder participation in agricultural policy-making process, and have these improved pro-poor policy outcomes?
- What are the most pressing constraints to effective farmer representation in agricultural policy formulation processes and how can these be overcome?
- What is 'best practice' when designing models for smallholder farmer participation in policy-making at national and regional platforms?

Overview of chapters

This book is divided into two sections: Section 1 – entitled 'Investment to boost smallholder farmer productivity' – comprises four chapters that discuss issues highlighted in sub-themes 1 and 2 on the trends and priorities for investment in smallholder agriculture across sub-Saharan Africa.

Chapter 1 is a broad analysis of areas of priority for investments that are required to transform smallholder agriculture in southern Africa into a means of lifting the millions of people who depend on this economic activity out of poverty. This chapter highlights the potential role of investments to improve access to credit, irrigation and infrastructure, as well as current trends in investment to support smallholder agriculture in the region and how effective these have been in different countries; and lastly it presents areas of investment in agriculture and rural development that offer the best returns and looks at how these have been affected by the socioeconomic context.

Chapter 2 focuses on some of these discussions, using the case of Malawi to highlight recent trends in investment to develop smallholder agriculture. This chapter discusses some of the underlying factors behind observed budgetary trends in Malawi and some of the strategies to improve the targeting of benefits meant for smallholder farmers. Chapter 3 follows up on these discussions, exploring the trends in agricultural financing in Tanzania, and the complexity of effective targeting and public expenditure tracking at the micro levels. Chapter 4 concludes Section 1 with a discussion of spending priorities for South Africa's smallholder agriculture. The author questions the potential benefits of incremental improvements in funding for smallholder agriculture given evidence of poorly conceived projects such as the land reform programme.

Section 2, entitled 'Enhancing smallholder farmer participation in agricultural development', is based on sub-theme 3 issues. Chapter 5 gives a regional perspective on stakeholder participation in policy processes, citing examples from southern and East Africa. The authors make a case for improving organisational capacity of farmer organisations in the sub-region to ensure effective representation of smallholder farmers in policy forums. Chapter 6 focuses on southern Africa, exploring the policy-making environment in the region and highlighting the potential role of legitimate, capable and professional farmer organisations in ensuring effective participation in policy formulation and advocacy. Chapter 7 uses the example of Tanzania to review models of stakeholder participation in policy-making and how these have been effective in the crafting of more inclusive policy outcomes.

Chapter 8 distils the key messages highlighted in the various chapters, reconciling some of the contentious debates that are typical throughout the book. The conclusion uses evidence from the chapters to revisit some of the overarching issues and questions raised in the themes, and provides more grounded responses and insights.

Conclusion

The lack of commitment to support adequate investment in agriculture has persisted despite numerous continent-wide and regional protocols by African governments and their development partners. This has left many doubting the adequacy of these measures and the political will to adhere to these agreements. For instance, at the Maputo Summit, African leaders agreed to devote at least 10 per cent of their public expenditure to agriculture with the aim of attaining agricultural growth rates of about 6 per cent annually. Few countries have been able to meet these targets and progress towards these has been limited.

The benefits of agricultural investments have been well documented. Recent studies confirm that agricultural spending generally has the largest positive effects on growth and poverty reduction, given the sector's strong linkages with other sectors. In many cases government agricultural spending has contributed substantially to agricultural productivity, rural household income, rural household consumption and rural poverty reduction. For instance, for each unit of local currency spent on the agricultural sector, 10 local currency units, on average, are earned in terms of increased agricultural productivity or income according to studies conducted in several African countries. These cost-benefit ratios are comparable to those obtained for India and Thailand, and nearly twice as large as those obtained for China. The evidence suggests that public investments on agriculture have substantially reduced rural poverty by stimulating agricultural growth and reducing food prices. Investments in other key facets of the rural economy, such as road infrastructure and education, were also shown to have large positive outcomes depending on the local context. These findings also suggest that the 'how' of agricultural spending can be as important as the 'how much' and that the organisation and governance of agricultural policy-making influence the productivity of expenditures undertaken in support of the sector.

Changing the face of African agriculture will require a change in mindset, not only on the part of political leadership but also the farmers themselves and civil society in general. Most African governments have clearly not prioritised agricultural transformation and continue to treat smallholder agriculture as just a way of life for a peasant population, with little to contribute towards economic growth and poverty alleviation. The farmers have also remained poorly organised, which undermines their voice to lobby for an adequate share of public resources. As such farmer groups and other civil society stakeholders remain marginal to processes of public expenditure planning and priority setting, leaving the fate of African agriculture to political goodwill rather than the needs and aspirations of the smallholder farmers themselves. Purposeful and sustained engagement of these stakeholders is required to unlock the potential of smallholder agriculture as the best option for transforming the lives of large numbers of poor households in rural communities across Africa, who would otherwise have limited economic opportunities to sustain themselves, let alone escape poverty.

Agricultural growth and priorities for investment in smallholder agriculture: Sub-Saharan Africa

LOVEMORE RUGUBE AND CHARLES MACHETHE

Introduction

Sub-Saharan Africa is home to approximately 229 million extremely poor, rural people, and agriculture is much more than simply food security to this population. Agriculture in sub-Sahara Africa provides about 1.3 billion jobs for smallholder farmers and landless workers, employing about 65 per cent of the labour force. It generates about 32 per cent of GDP growth, and GDP growth from agriculture is about four times more effective in reducing poverty than GDP originating outside the agricultural sector (World Development Bank). Sub-Saharan Africa (SSA) has the highest levels of poverty and hunger and the worst human development outcomes of any region in the world (World Development Indicators 2004). Agriculture accounts for about 30 per cent of sub-Saharan Africa's GDP, and for at least 40 per cent of its export value. The majority of the poor and hungry in sub-Sahara Africa live in rural areas and essentially depend on agriculture. Most of the region's populations depend on smallholder farming for their livelihoods. Sub-Saharan Africa is the only region in the world in which poverty is on the increase and per capita food production is declining. Alleviating poverty in most agrarian economies, including countries in which the contribution of agriculture to GDP is relatively low, requires the development of smallholder agriculture.

Smallholder farmers face several barriers and challenges both for domestic production and production for export. Access to credit is just one of these, and has long been a key barrier to production for smallholders, undermining their ability to invest in their farms and production, often leading to declining levels of productivity. Investment in agriculture is necessary to ensure rapid economic growth and poverty reduction in the region. Many of the key investments required to accelerate agricultural growth, such as technological research, rural infrastructure, education, market access, organisation and enforcement, are public investments. Although private sector involvement in this sector is more important than ever, particularly with regard to services such as finance and marketing, the private sector has not invested sufficiently to ensure broad-based agricultural growth because these investments are considered to be insufficiently profitable. The public sector needs to provide the necessary research, transport and market infrastructure necessary to stimulate agricultural growth.

Many governments and donor countries are beginning to tap into the vast potential of agriculture in sub-Saharan Africa and are making new investments in the sector to enhance economic opportunities and increase food security. The United Nations has argued that access to credit and financial services is more important than before in the context of the international financial crisis which has resulted in declining remittances, which serve as an important safety-net for much of the world's poor. For many large businesses who source from smallholders in the developing world, sustainability concerns (related in particular to climate change) are driving projects to ensure that smallholder production is economically, socially and environmentally sustainable.

This chaper presents details on the form of investments needed to prioritise and transform smallholder agriculture in sub-Saharan Africa in order to reduce poverty and hunger. Firstly, it addresses the question of whether smallholder agriculture provides realistic opportunities for rural populations to lift themselves out of poverty. Secondly, it presents the current trends in investment in smallholder agriculture and looks at how effective these investments have been in the various countries of the region. Lastly, it discusses which areas of investment offer the best returns and how these have been affected by the socioeconomic context.

Smallholder agriculture as a vehicle to poverty reduction for the rural populations in sub-Saharan Africa

Africa is the only continent with agricultural potential that is not being used effectively. Food shortages and the impact of the oil price on the cost of imported food made African governments realise that they could no longer afford to ignore the agricultural potential of their countries. They recognise that increasing government spending on agriculture is a fundamental prerequisite for achieving a 6 per cent annual growth rate in agricultural GDP – a goal adopted by NEPAD through the Comprehensive African Agriculture Development Programme (CAADP). This is evident in the Maputo Declaration, in which African leaders called for a 10 per cent budget allocation to agriculture by 2008, as part of the commitment to the Millennium Development Goals (MDG1) and (CAADP) goals. These well-intended efforts have generated debate within international development communities about the level and utilisation of resources, given that agriculture is a neglected sector, affected by droughts, insecurity and unfavorable policies towards smallholder farmers.

More than 80 per cent of the decline in worldwide rural poverty from 1993 to 2002 was attributed to agriculture. The important role that smallholder agriculture can play in reducing poverty and serving as an engine for growth was demonstrated throughout the Green Revolution in Asia, particularly in India and China. SADC countries cannot bypass this development pathway, as the majority of their populations live in rural areas. Recent evidence from International Food Policy Research Institute (IFPRI) showed that promoting higher agricultural growth is key to reducing poverty, promoting overall economic growth and achieving MDG1, which is to halve the number of poor people by 2015 (Diao *et al.*, 2007).

There are a range of instruments that governments and donors can use to promote the required growth in smallholder agriculture in sub-Saharan Africa. Government spending is one of the most direct and efficient methods, yet agricultural spending remains low when compared with that in other developing regions. Sub-Saharan Africa still spends only 4–5 per cent of its total budget on agriculture compared with 8–14 per cent in Asia. During the Green Revolution in Asia this share was even larger, upwards of 15 per cent. Agricultural expenditure is a more appropriate measure of a government's support for agriculture as it measures agricultural spending relative to the size of the sector rather than the total budget.

With the right kind of policy and investments, smallholder farmers can make valuable contributions to the growth of their countries. In many cases they are the only available engine for growth, and for dealing with rural poverty and social aspects of the population at large. Agricultural growth may lower food prices and thus provide cheaper wage goods, which stimulates industrial growth: however, if the economy is open to international trade, prices will not fall below international levels and the benefit may not materialise. Increases in yield have the potential to lift a large number of individuals out of poverty – specifically, a yield increase of one-third might reduce the numbers in poverty by a quarter or more. The challenges faced by smallholder farmers are firstly, the decline in prices for major export commodities (cocoa, coffee, cotton, palm oil, tea), which has been compounded by the rising costs of farm inputs. Secondly, the trend towards globalisation, which in theory should give small farmers access to lucrative markets, is likely to spell death for many small farmers, who will lose much of their urban markets to imported goods from other countries. Strategies of labour-intensive technical progress and the distribution of land and human capital not only reduce poverty in the short run, but also ease the transition from agriculture-based to more broad-based poverty reduction.

Agricultural growth performance in the SADC region

This chapter reviews the performance of the 15 SADC member states against several sector-wide indicators, including total GDP, agricultural GDP, and underlying agricultural productivity (as captured by yields and production of major crops and livestock, and the consumption of fertiliser). The aim is not only to dissect each indicator country-by-country, but also to present region-wide trends while shedding light on important differences across countries. The emerging trends provide a basis for assessing SADC's success in achieving key targets set out in MDG1, and by the CAADP and SADC-RISDP plans. This assessment has been done by quantifying the gaps between the observed trends of the relevant variables and corresponding targets. Major divergences are evident across the region. The ratios between the gaps and divergences are computed to give an indication of the required reduction or growth needed to meet the targets.

Economic growth and gross domestic product (GDP)

In 2008, the combined regional GDP stood at US$274 billion, while the average regional per capita GDP stood at approximately US$1,790 (2000–2008). Using GDP per capita income as the proxy of the level of development, 8 of 15 SADC countries fell below the low-income countries' IMF classification over the period. These included DRC, Lesotho, Madagascar, Malawi, Mozambique, Tanzania, Zambia and Zimbabwe. Angola, Namibia, Swaziland, Botswana, Mauritius and South Africa fell in the middle-income bracket. South Africa's GDP in 2008 was US$183 billion, making it more than twice as large as the GDP of all other SADC countries combined (Table 1.1).

Shares of regional GDP have been relatively stable since 1990, with only strife-torn Zimbabwe and the DRC showing significant reductions, and Angola registering a significant post-conflict increase (Table 1.2). Overall, GDP growth in the SADC region has been impressive since 2003, averaging well over 5 per cent per year, slightly higher than the continent-wide growth rate (Table 1.3). Nine of the SADC countries registered growth rates of 5 per cent or higher in 2005–2008, with Angola, Malawi and Mozambique performing exceptionally well. Botswana, Mauritius, Swaziland and Zimbabwe were the low performers by regional trends.

Table 1.1: Trends in GDP in SADC countries (1990−2008)
GDP (constant 2000 US$ billion)

	1990	2000	2003	2005	2007	2008
Angola	8.5	9.1	11.1	14.9	21.3	24.5
Botswana	3.4	6.2	7.1	8.0	8.5	8.5
Congo DR	7.7	4.3	4.6	5.3	6.0	6.3
Lesotho	0.5	0.8	0.9	0.9	1.0	1.1
Madagascar	3.3	3.9	3.9	4.3	4.8	5.2
Malawi	1.2	1.7	1.7	1.8	2.1	2.4
Mauritius	2.7	4.5	5.0	5.5	5.9	6.3
Mozambique	2.5	4.2	5.5	6.4	7.5	7.9
Namibia	2.6	3.9	4.3	5.0	5.5	5.7
Seychelles	0.4	0.6	0.6	0.6	0.7	0.7
South Africa	110.9	132.9	145.9	160.6	177.8	183.2
Swaziland	1.0	1.5	1.6	1.7	1.8	1.8
Tanzania	6.8	9.1	10.9	12.5	14.3	15.4
Zambia	3.0	3.2	3.7	4.1	4.6	4.9
Zimbabwe	6.7	7.4	6.2	5.6	0.0	0.0
SADC	161.3	193.3	213.1	237.3	262.0	273.8
SSA	273.6	342.3	381.0	426.7	481.7	505.9

Source: World bank (2009)

Table 1.2: Country's contributions (%) to the region's GDP

	1990	2000	2003	2005	2007	2008
Angola	5.2	4.7	5.2	6.3	8.1	8.9
Botswana	2.1	3.2	3.4	3.4	3.3	3.1
Congo DR	4.7	2.2	2.2	2.2	2.3	2.3
Lesotho	0.3	0.4	0.4	0.4	0.4	0.4
Madagascar	2.0	2.0	1.8	1.8	1.8	1.9
Malawi	0.8	0.9	0.8	0.8	0.8	0.9
Mauritius	1.7	2.3	2.3	2.3	2.3	2.3
Mozambique	1.5	2.2	2.6	2.7	2.8	2.9
Namibia	1.6	2.0	2.0	2.1	2.1	2.1
Seychelles	0.2	0.3	0.3	0.3	0.3	0.3
South Africa	68.8	68.7	68.5	67.7	67.9	66.9
Swaziland	0.6	0.8	0.7	0.7	0.7	0.7
Tanzania	4.2	4.7	5.1	5.3	5.5	5.6
Zambia	1.9	1.7	1.7	1.7	1.8	1.8
Zimbabwe	4.2	3.8	2.9	2.4	0.0	0.0

Source: World bank (2009)

Table 1.3: Trends in annual GDP growth rates of SADC countries (1990-2008) Compunded average annual growth (%) rate in GDP

	1990 – 2000	2000 – 2003	2003 – 2005	2005 – 2008
Angola	0.8	6.9	15.8	17.9
Botswana	6.2	4.9	5.6	2.0
Congo DR	−5.6	2.3	7.3	6.0
Lesotho	3.8	2.9	2.6	5.7
Madagascar	1.7	0.5	4.9	6.0
Malawi	3.4	−1.2	4.1	38.8
Mauritius	5.3	3.8	4.6	4.5
Mozambique	5.5	8.9	8.1	7.4
Namibia	4.2	3.4	7.3	4.6
Seychelles	4.5	−2.4	2.2	6.1
South Africa	1.8	3.2	4.9	4.5
Swaziland	3.7	2.2	2.4	3.0
Tanzania	2.9	6.4	7.1	7.1
Zambia	0.7	4.4	5.3	6.1
Zimbabwe	0.9	-5.9	-4.6	-5.3
SADC	1.8	3.3	5.5	4.9

Source: World bank (2009)

Agricultural GDP

Agriculture accounts for more than 20 per cent of national GDP in five SADC countries – DRC, Madagascar, Malawi, Mozambique, Tanzania and Zambia (Table 1.4) – an indicator of the relative importance of the agricultural sector in the economies of the low-income countries of southern Africa. The average share of agriculture in regional GDP, excluding South Africa, is 13.7 per cent. This contribution drops to 12.8 per cent when South Africa is included. The six SADC countries in which agriculture accounts for more than 20 per cent of GDP together produce 76 per cent of the region's agricultural value added. Tanzania has the region's largest agricultural sector, having overtaken South Africa between 2000 and 2008 (Tables 1.5 and 1.6). Agriculture in South Africa is small relative to other sectors, but it is still larger than the rest of SADC countries.

Table 1.4: Trends in the share of agriculture in GDP in SADC countries (1990–2008)

Agriculture value added (% of GDP)

	1990	2000	2003	2005	2007	2008
Angola	17.9	5.7	8.3	7.7	9.7	10.1
Botswana	4.9	2.4	2.4	2.0	1.8	1.7
Congo DR	31.0	50.0	51.0	44.7	41.1	–
Lesotho	23.2	11.7	9.5	7.9	7.4	7.2
Madagascar	28.6	29.2	29.2	28.3	26.2	25.2
Malawi	45.0	39.5	37.6	32.9	34.3	34.3
Mauritius	13.1	5.9	6.1	6.1	5.3	4.5
Mozambique	37.1	24.0	28.0	27.0	27.6	28.3
Namibia	11.7	11.8	10.9	11.3	10.3	8.0
Seychelles	4.8	3.0	3.0	2.5	2.4	2.3
South Africa	4.6	3.3	3.6	2.7	3.2	2.8
Swaziland	10.4	12.5	9.6	8.5	7.3	8.1
Tanzania	46.0	45.0	45.0	46.1	–	–
Zambia	20.6	22.3	22.6	22.1	21.6	21.2
Zimbabwe	16.5	18.5	16.8	19.1	–	–
SADC incl SA	21.0	19.0	18.9	17.9	15.2	12.8
SADC excl SA	22.0	20.1	20.0	19.0	16.2	13.7
SSA	18.8	342.3	381.0	426.7	481.7	505.9

Source: World Bank (2009)

Table 1.5: Trends in agricultural GDP in SADC countries (1990—2008)
Agricultural GDP (constant 2000 US$ million)

	1990	2000	2003	2005	2007	2008
Angola	685.9	517.1	766.8	1,023.7	1,367.1	1,739.8
Botswana	154.7	139.2	146.7	130.0	131.7	134.3
Congo DR	2,011.1	2,125.7	2,077.6	2,150.0	2,270.4	2,338.5
Lesotho	89.1	86.1	69.6	63.1	66.3	66.0
Madagascar	859.8	1,026.3	1,067.4	1,127.6	1,177.2	1,209.9
Malawi	301.6	621.7	568.1	534.5	633.7	666.5
Mauritius	273.8	230.3	269.4	288.3	275.5	258.9
Mozambique	686.6	887.2	1,141.1	1,272.8	1,504.8	1,610.8
Namibia	277.5	420.9	450.0	479.8	469.7	662.4
Seychelles	18.4	18.4	17.2	16.9	18.9	20.0
South Africa	3,691.6	3,955.6	3,991.4	4,267.3	3,968.0	4,006.8
Swaziland	142.5	152.8	154.6	158.2	158.9	163.3
Tanzania	2,766.6	3,773.0	4,345.6	4,833.9	–	–
Zimbabwe	857.9	1173.9	863.3	754.4	–	–
SADC incl SA	13,288.7	15,771.7	12,777.6	17,771.6	12,777.6	13,636.8
SADC excl SA	9,597.1	11,816.1	8,809.6	13,504.4	8,809.6	9,630.1

Data source: World Bank (2009)

Table 1.6: Country contributions to SADC agricultural GDP (1990—2008)
Contribution to SADC agricultural GDP

	1990	2000	2003	2005	2006	2007	2008
Angola	5.2	3.3	6.0	5.8	6.5	10.7	12.8
Botswana	1.2	0.9	1.1	0.7	0.8	1.0	1.0
Congo DR	15.1	13.5	16.3	12.1	12.8	17.8	17.1
Lesotho	0.7	0.5	0.5	0.4	0.4	0.5	0.5
Madagascar	6.5	6.5	8.4	6.3	6.7	9.2	8.9
Malawi	2.3	3.9	4.4	3.0	3.5	5.0	4.9
Mauritius	2.1	1.5	2.1	1.6	1.6	2.2	1.9
Mozambique	5.2	5.6	8.9	7.2	8.2	11.8	11.8
Namibia	2.1	2.7	3.5	2.7	2.8	3.7	4.9
Seychelles	0.1	0.1	0.1	0.1	0.1	0.1	0.1
South Africa	27.8	25.1	31.2	24.0	22.8	31.1	29.4
Swaziland	1.1	1.0	1.2	0.9	0.9	1.2	1.2
Tanzania	20.8	23.9	34.0	27.2	29.1	–	0.0
Zambia	3.5	4.1	5.1	3.8	4.0	5.8	5.6
Zimbabwe	6.5	7.4	6.8	4.2	0.0	–	0.0
SADC incl SA	100.0	100.0	100.0	100.0	100.0	100.0	100.0

Data source: World Bank (2009)

With the four exceptions that tend to pull up the regional average (Angola, Malawi, Mozambique and Namibia), SADC's agricultural sector has performed poorly in the recent past (2005–2008) (Table 1.7). It is worth noting, however, that Angola and Mozambique are starting from a very low base and that Malawi has been implementing a very rigorous agricultural subsidy, which probably explains its remarkable performance. For the period 2005 to 2008, agriculture in Mauritius, South Africa and Zimbabwe registered negative growth. Botswana registered negative growth previously (2003–2005) but reversed the trend in 2005–2008, albeit only to relatively low levels.

Table 1.7: Trends in annual agricultural growth rates of SADC countries (1990–2008) Compounded average annual growth in agricultural GDP (%)

	1990–2000	2000–2003	2003–2005	2005–2008
Angola	−2.8	14.0	15.5	19.3
Botswana	−1.1	1.8	−5.9	1.1
Congo DR	−5.6	2.3	7.3	6.0
Lesotho	−0.3	−6.8	−4.8	1.5
Madagascar	1.8	1.3	2.8	2.4
Malawi	7.5	−3.0	−3.0	7.6
Mauritius	−1.7	5.4	3.4	−3.5
Mozambique	2.6	8.8	5.6	8.2
Namibia	4.3	2.3	3.3	11.4
Seychelles	0.0	−2.4	−0.8	5.9
South Africa	0.7	0.3	3.4	−2.1
Swaziland	0.7	0.4	1.2	1.1
Tanzania	3.2	4.8	5.5	–
Zambia	3.2	0.2	1.8	4.2
Zimbabwe	3.2	−9.7	-6.5	–
SADC incl SA	1.7	1.7	3.5	−8.4
SADC excl SA	2.1	2.1	3.6	−10.5
SSA	2.8	2.2	4.1	4.2

Data source: World Bank (2009)

Progress towards 6 per cent CAADP growth target

Under CAADP, SADC member countries committed themselves to achieving 6 per cent annual growth rates in agricultural GDP. However, countries have achieved different levels of progress (Table 1.8). Taking 2000–2008 as a base, the target of a 6 per cent growth rate in agGDP has been achieved only by Angola, Malawi, Mozambique and Namibia (Table 1.8). To reach this target, SADC as a whole needs to raise growth rates by 2 per cent or more. DRC, Lesotho, Madagascar, Swaziland and Zimbabwe need to increase growth by more than 3 per cent.

Table 1.8: Progress towards achieving 6% agricultural GDP growth: CAADP growth target

	Compounded average annual growth in agricultural GDP (%)			
	1990–2000	2000–2003	2003–2005	2005–2008
Angola	−2.8	14.0	15.5	19.3
Botswana	−1.1	1.8	−5.9	1.1
Congo DR	−5.6	2.3	7.3	6.0
Lesotho	−0.3	−6.8	−4.8	1.5
Madagascar	1.8	1.3	2.8	2.4
Malawi	7.5	−3.0	−3.0	7.6
Mauritius	−1.7	5.4	3.4	−3.5
Mozambique	2.6	8.8	5.6	8.2
Namibia	4.3	2.3	3.3	11.4
Seychelles	0.0	−2.4	−0.8	5.9
South Africa	0.7	0.3	3.4	−2.1
Swaziland	0.7	0.4	1.2	1.1
Tanzania	3.2	4.8	5.5	3.8
Zambia	3.2	0.2	1.8	4.2
Zimbabwe	3.2	−9.7	−6.5	−10.0
SADC incl SA	1.7	1.7	3.5	−8.4
SADC excl SA	2.1	2.1	3.6	−10.5
SSA	2.8	2.2	4.1	4.2

Data source: World Bank (2009)

Progress towards achieving the SADC-RISDP 7 per cent GDP growth target

Taking 2000–2008 as a base, Angola, Malawi, Mozambique and Tanzania were again the only countries achieving the target (see Table 1.9 on the following page). A positive correlation between agricultural and economic growth in these countries is evident in these tables.

Underlying agricultural productivity

The poor aggregate performance of the region's agricultural sector is grounded in sluggish growth in underlying agricultural productivity, which is largely a result of insufficient investment in agriculture, poor access to agricultural inputs (especially fertilisers and improved seeds), poor access to markets and low levels of technological development and use. Other factors explaining the underlying low productivity include adverse climatic conditions and HIV/AIDS, which threaten the livelihoods of farming households. In the period between 1990 and 2007, per capita food production increased in only three countries: Angola, Tanzania, and Malawi (Table 1.10).

Table 1.9: Progress towards achieving the 7% GDP growth: SADC-RISDP target.
Compunded average annual growth (%) rate in GDP

	1990−2000	2000−2003	2003−2005	2005−2008
Angola	0.8	6.9	15.8	17.9
Botswana	6.2	4.9	5.6	2.0
Congo DR	−5.6	2.3	7.3	6.0
Lesotho	3.8	2.9	2.6	5.7
Madagascar	1.7	0.5	4.9	6.0
Malawi	3.4	−1.2	4.1	8.8
Mauritius	5.3	3.8	4.6	4.5
Mozambique	5.5	8.9	8.1	7.4
Namibia	4.2	3.4	7.3	4.6
Seychelles	4.5	−2.4	2.2	6.1
South Africa	1.8	3.2	4.9	4.5
Swaziland	3.7	2.2	2.4	3.0
Tanzania	2.9	6.4	7.1	7.1
Zambia	0.7	4.4	5.3	6.1
Zimbabwe	0.9	−5.9	−4.6	−5.3
SADC	1.8	3.3	5.5	4.9
SSA	2.3	3.6	5.8	5.8

Data source: World Bank (2009)

Table 1.10: Trends in index of per capita food production in SADC countries (1990–2007).
Index of food production per capita

	1990	2000	2003	2005	2006	2007
Angola	81	99	120	129	128	125
Botswana	137	99	99	106	103	102
Congo DR	159	99	89	84	86	78
Lesotho	110	101	86	87	67	82
Madagascar	126	99	90	102	101	99
Malawi	59	101	91	76	102	115
Mauritius	107	101	106	103	99	95
Mozambique	101	95	97	99	95	84
Namibia	131	97	97	95	92	90
Sychelles	85	100	97	90	91	91
South Africa	108	105	100	106	102	101
Swaziland	128	99	104	111	104	101
Tanzania	116	96	97	110	115	112
Zambia	111	100	105	103	107	101
Zimbabwe	108	105	85	77	82	78

Source: FAO (2009)

Current trends in investment to support smallholder agriculture

Historically, agricultural spending in Africa has been very low compared with other developing regions. As mentioned earlier, African public spending on agriculture between 1980 and 2005 accounted for 5 to 7 per cent of the total national budget, whereas agricultural allocations in Asia were between 6 and 15 per cent. As a percentage of agGDP, African agricultural spending was only half that of Asia in 2005. In an effort to address this situation, African heads of state adopted the Maputo Declaration on Agriculture and Food Security in 2003, committing their countries to allocate at least 10 per cent of national budgetary resources to the agricultural sector. This level of investment in agriculture was deemed necessary to support an annual growth rate of 6 per cent set by NEPAD through its Comprehensive Africa Agriculture Development Programme (CAADP) on food security and poverty reduction.

For a variety of reasons, many of the African countries have not been able to meet these targets. At issue is the level and composition of public expenditures devoted to the region's agricultural sectors and how this has influenced agricultural performance.

A SADC-wide perspective

Using the Growth Poverty Elasticity methodology, sub-Saharan African countries will need to boost their annual agricultural growth to 7.5 per cent per year in order to achieve MDG1. To reach this target, government agricultural spending will have to increase to US$13.7 billion per year (Table 1.11). If these countries are to fulfil their commitments to allocate 10 per cent of their budgets to agriculture under the Maputo Declaration, the MDG1 target would require additional or incremental spending of US$4.8 billion per year.

Southern African countries will also need to boost their annual agricultural growth to 7.5 per cent per year to achieve MDG1. To reach this target, government agricultural spending will have to increase to US$0.8 billion per year (Table 1.11). If southern African countries are to fulfil their commitments to allocate 10 per cent of their budgets to agriculture under the Maputo Declaration, the MDG1 target would require additional or incremental spending of US$0.04 billion per year.

Table 1.11: Annual total agricultural spending (US$ billion in 2008) required to meet MDG1 in sub-Saharan Africa and southern Africa

	sub-Saharan Africa	Southern Africa
Total	13.7	0.8
Additional/incremental	4.8	0.04

Source: IFPR Policy Brief (2008)

Maputo Declaration

Most countries in the region have yet to achieve the Maputo Declaration target of allocating 10 per cent of public expenditure to the agricultural sector (Table 1.12). Only Malawi has consistently exceeded the target in recent years following a government input subsidy programme. Despite this rather disappointing trend, it is encouraging that between 2003 and 2007, all but four SADC countries (Lesotho, Mozambique, Swaziland and Zimbabwe) increased their allocations to agriculture. Prior to 2005, Zimbabwe's share was only slightly below the target, but since then it has fallen sharply as a direct result of political and economic strife.

Deviations from the 10 per cent target vary widely across the region. On average the SADC region needs an increase in public expenditure on agriculture of about 5 per cent to reach the target. Eight countries need increases larger than 5 per cent. Botswana, DRC and Mauritius face the greatest challenge as they need percentage increases of between 7 and 9 per cent. Ongoing political instability in the DRC has taken its toll on the country's focus on the agricultural sector. Despite consistent and significant economic progress in Botswana, the agricultural sector has been neglected perhaps in favour of the dominant and highly-lucrative mining sector.

Table 1.12. shows the share of agricultural expenditure in national budgets. It shows that progress in meeting the 10 per cent allocation of national budgets to agriculture has not been achieved in most countries in the SADC, with the exception of Malawi, Mozambique and Tanzania. Governments need to commit themselves to the target to achieve the growth rate required to reduce poverty and hunger by 2015.

Table 1.12: Share of agricultural expenditure in national budgets

	03—04	04—05	05—06	06—07	07—08	08—09	09—10	10—11
Angola	-	2.2	6.5	5.3	-	-	-	-
Botswana	2.8	2.7	3.2	3.3	-	-	-	-
Congo DR	0.8	0.7	1.5	1.8	-	-	-	-
Lesotho	4.8	5.0	4.0	3.5	-	-	-	-
Madagascar	8.0	7.9	8.0	8.0	-	-	-	-
Malawi	6.6	12.7	11.0	13.2	14	13	15	
Mauritius	2.7	3.4	2.9	2.9	-	-	-	-
Mozambique	6.2	4.4	3.4	3.9	4.9	7.4	-	
Namibia	7.3	6.9	8.2	8.0	-	-	-	-
South Africa	-	-	-	-	2.4	2.1	2.3	2.2
Swaziland	5.0	6.0	4.7	3.7	-	-	-	-
Tanzania	5.7	4.7	5.8	5.8	6.2	6.4	-	
Zambia	1.8	3.2	3.6	4.0	8.5	5.8	-	
Zimbabwe	9.4	10.0	6.2	6.0	-	-	-	-
SADC	5.1	5.4	5.3	5.3	-	-	-	-

Source: Author's computations 2010

Table 1.13: Required percentage increases in public expenditure on agriculture to achieve the targets of NEPAD/CAADP of 10% (base = 2003–2007)

Angola	5.6%
Botswana	7.0%
DRC	8.8%
Lesotho	5.7%
Madagascar	3.0%
Malawi	−0.9%
Mauritius	6.9%
Mozambique	5.5%
Namibia	2.4%
Seychelles	9.0%
Swaziland	5.2%
Tanzania	4.5%
Zambia	5.0%
Zimbabwe	1.5%
SADC	4.9%

Source: Author's computation

Malawi: A success story?

Agriculture is the single most important sector of the Malawian economy, contributing approximately 39 per cent of the country's GDP and employing up to 80 per cent of the work-force. Close to 80 per cent of export earnings also come from the agricultural sector. For the country's rural population, which makes up close to 75 per cent of the poor in the country, agriculture contributes significantly to household food security and is the basis for most economic activities. Despite its central role, agriculture in Malawi has been characterised by low and stagnant yields and high fluctuations in production volumes. High dependence on rain-fed systems and the associated low levels of irrigation development increases vulnerability to weather-related shocks. Low uptake of improved farm inputs and other yield-enhancing technologies, poor infrastructure and a failing extension support system have also been cited as reasons for the poor performance of the sector.

Since 2002, Malawi has embarked on a set of ambitious macroeconomic reforms under the Malawi Growth and Development Strategy (MGDS). These reforms are expected to lead to economic growth rates of around 6 per cent, resulting in significant poverty reduction. The MGDS recognises agriculture as a central facet of the economy and acknowledges that food security is a prerequisite for economic growth and poverty alleviation. The MGDS focuses on improving agricultural productivity and integrating smallholder farmers into mainstream commercial activity. In line with these broader national priorities, the Ministry of Agriculture and Food Security (MoAFS) formulated an Agricultural Development Programme (ADP) that guides public and private investment in the sector. Key areas that have seen improved investments include household food security, agro-processing and marketing, and sustainable land and water management.

Since 2003, Malawi's public expenditure on the agricultural sector has increased almost sevenfold (Figure 1.1), making Malawi the first country in the SADC region to achieve the CAADP target of allocating 10 per cent of its public expenditure to the agricultural sector.

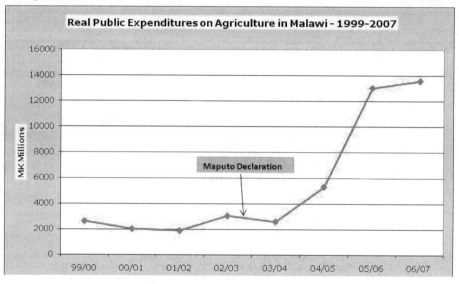

Figure 1.1:   Real public expenditure on agriculture in Malawi, 1999–2007

Data sources: Computed from various budget documents of Government of Malawi (GoM 1998a, 1998b, 1998c, 1998d, 2000, 2001, 2002, 2003, 2004a, 2004b, 2007a, 2007b, 2007c)

The composition of Malawi's agricultural expenditure has also changed significantly. In line with the food security focus, the livestock and crop sub-sector expenditure has increased substantially (Figure 1.2). In 2003 this sub-sector took up just over 70 per cent of the agricultural budget. By 2006 this had increased to nearly 95 per cent of the total agriculture budget, with forestry and fisheries sharing the remaining 5 per cent. This trend confirms a deliberate effort to improve crop and livestock productivity as suggested in the ADP strategy by the MoAFS.

Analysis of Malawi's agriculture budget by programmes is complicated by the frequent changes in the allocation of major projects and initiatives across programmes. Especially problematic is the 'Administration and Support' category, which includes a large 'development' component. Also included in the category, under the 'Nutrition and Food Security Programme' are major subsidy initiatives such as the Targeted Input Programme and Starter Pack Programme, as well as support to parastatal agencies such as the Agricultural Development and Marketing Corporation (ADMARC) and the National Food Reserve Agency. The Administration and Support Programme had been in decline since 2000, but between 2004 and 2006

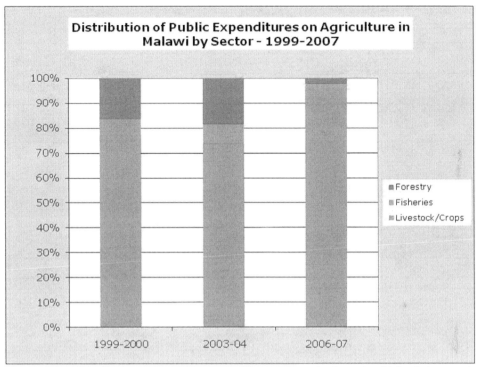

Figure 1.2: Distribution of public expenditure on agriculture in Malawi by sector, 1999—2007

Data sources: Computed from various budget documents of Government of Malawi (GoM 1998a, 1998b, 1998c, 1998d, 2000, 2001, 2002, 2003, 2004a, 2004b, 2007a, 2007b, 2007c)

it saw a dramatic tenfold increase. Malawi's success in achieving the target of the Maputo Declaration for expenditure on agriculture presents a unique opportunity to understand the challenges and opportunities facing other SADC countries as they strive towards this target.

This Nutrition and Food Security Programme appeared as a distinct development budget item in the 2004/05 fiscal year, when it accounted for 42 per cent of the spending in crop and livestock development projects. However, its share of total (recurrent and development projects) spending rose from 39 per cent in 2004/05 to 41 per cent in 2005/06, and stood at 55 per cent in 2006/07 (Table 1.14). Without this programme, between 2004 and 2007, agriculture's share of Malawi's budget would have ranged between 3.6 and 8.1 per cent, rather than being between 11 and 13.2 per cent. Clearly, some initiatives in the Nutrition and Food Security Programme are productivity- and growth-enhancing, for example, the Targeted Input Programme and Starter Pack Programme. But others would seem to be less so, for example, support to the National Food Reserve Agency. The latter could be imparting an upward bias on Malawi's reported share of expenditure on agriculture, clouding assessments of the country's success in achieving the 10 per cent target set by the Maputo Declaration on a long-term basis.

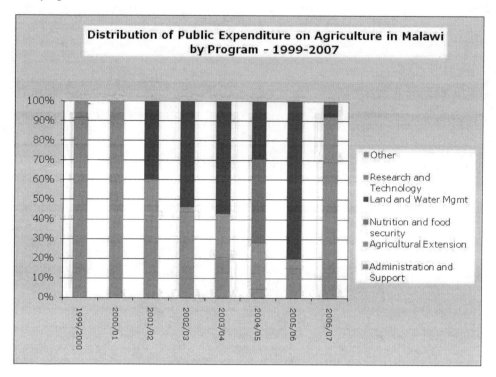

Figure 1.3: Distribution of public expenditure on agriculture in Malawi by programme, 1999—2007

Data sources: Computed from various budget documents of Government of Malawi (GoM 1998a, 1998b, 1998c, 1998d, 2000, 2001, 2002, 2003, 2004a, 2004b, 2007a, 2007b, 2007c)

Table 1.14: The share of the Nutrition and Food Security Programme in the agriculture budget of Malawi, 2004–2007

	2004–2005	2005–2006	2006–2007
Share	39.5	40.6	55.2

Data sources: Computed from various budget documents of Government of Malawi (GoM 1998a, 1998b, 1998c, 1998d, 2000, 2001, 2002, 2003, 2004a, 2004b, 2007a, 2007b, 2007c)

Table 1.15: Impact of the Nutrition and Food Security Programme on agricultural expenditure in Malawi, 2004–2007

	2004–2005	2005–2006	2006–2007
Without N&FS	3.4	4.3	6.0
With N&FS	5.3	13.0	13.6

Data sources: Computed from various budget documents of Government of Malawi (GoM 1998a, 1998b, 1998c, 1998d, 2000, 2001, 2002, 2003, 2004a, 2004b, 2007a, 2007b, 2007c)

Note: N&FS = Nutrition and Food Security

The recurrent budget supports normal operating costs, along with those associated with agricultural subsidy initiatives, ADMARC and the National Food Reserve Agency. The development budget supports investment in long-term assets such as irrigation infrastructure. In 2007, the recurrent share of Malawi's agriculture budget stood at almost 70 per cent, compared to 50 per cent in 1999; the 2007 development share was, therefore, well below its 1999 level, but it grew steadily between 2005 and 2007.

While the Malawian government assumed responsibility for almost three-quarters of the agriculture budget between 1999 and 2007, its development partners covered almost 90 per cent of the crucial development component.

Table 1.16: Government and donor shares of overall and development components of Malawi's agricultural budget, 1999–2007.

	Overall agriculture	Development
Donors	25.9	87.0
Government	74.1	13.0

Data sources: Computed from various budget documents of Government of Malawi (GoM 1998a, 1998b, 1998c, 1998d, 2000, 2001, 2002, 2003, 2004a, 2004b, 2007a, 2007b, 2007c)

Table 1.17: Share of 'development' spending in the agriculture budget in Malawi.

	99—00	00—01	01—02	02—03	03—04	04—05	05—06	06—07
Share	47.4	33.9	18.8	30.0	28.0	13.8	13.7	27.7

Data sources: Computed from various budget documents of Government of Malawi (GoM 1998a, 1998b, 1998c, 1998d, 2000, 2001, 2002, 2003, 2004a, 2004b, 2007a, 2007b, 2007c)

By devoting increasingly large shares of public resources to spur growth in the agriculture sector, Malawi is obviously a country that has made a strong commitment to agriculture. A number of potential lessons for other SADC countries emerge. The balance between 'productive' and 'safety net' components of the agriculture budget is not clear, but the steadily expanding development element suggests grounds for optimism that productive elements are receiving attention. Given Malawi's exposure to weather-related supply shocks, the need for vulnerability-reducing elements in the national budget is beyond dispute. Their potential for spurring growth in the agricultural sector has yet to be established, but their potential for protecting hard-won development gains should not be underestimated. The large share of recurrent expenditure in the budget is not ideal, but is also not unusual in a country at Malawi's stage of overall development. The division of labour between the government and its development partners appears sensible in the short term.

Suggested priorities for investment in smallholder agriculture and rural development

Develop supply capacity in smallholder production

African agriculture is in crisis, the CAADP affirms, and that situation 'demands a crisis response'. Although urbanisation is increasing rapidly, agriculture still provides livelihoods for about 60 per cent of the continent's active labour force, contributes 17 per cent of Africa's total GDP and accounts for 40 per cent of its foreign currency earnings. Sustainable intensification of smallholder agriculture is crucial to create the necessary surplus for the market. Smallholder farmers need access to appropriate technologies and support services to effectively participate in the transformation process. The agricultural research and development (R&D) system has been undergoing a series of transformations over the years. To make poverty-reducing, broad-based agricultural growth possible, it is important to invest in institutions that provide agricultural services (especially extension and rural finance) and to develop input supply systems and reliable local output markets. Creating an environment that enables collective action among farm households in the form of credit groups and producer associations is also important to address market failures more effectively. When agricultural production takes off, the trans-action volumes for inputs, outputs and services increase, and farmers learn how to use and adapt new technologies. Hence, the reasons that gave rise to market fail-ures in the food staple sector are less relevant, and state intervention in these areas should be withdrawn. Farmers' yields have essentially stagnated for decades. The reasons for this are multiple, says the CAADP: continuing dependence on uncertain rainfall, nutritional deficiencies in Africa's soils, small farms and a lack of research and appropriate technology. Research shows that a 1 per cent increase in agricul-tural yields decreases the percentage of population living on less than US$1 a day by 0.64 to 0.91 per cent, with a slightly higher reduction for Africa. According to the World Bank, a 10 per cent increase in crop yields leads to a 9 per cent decrease in the percentage of people living on less than US$1 a day. The same effect is not achieved by growth in the manufacturing and service sectors.

Much can be done to increase African farm yields through simple methods of improving soil fertility and better utilising the continent's available water. Currently, only 12.6 million hectares of agricultural land are under managed systems of water and land development. The vast bulk of farmland is left to the vagaries of weather, including insufficient rainfall and flooding that may strip away top soils, as well as unsustainable farming methods that gradually deplete soil nutrients. Some 874 million ha of land are deemed suitable for agriculture, but 83 per cent of this is subject to serious limitations such as poor soil fertility. About 16 per cent of Africa's soils are categorised as 'low nutrient', compared with just 4 per cent in Asia. Each year, the depletion of existing soil nutrients brings crop losses estimated at between US$1 billion and US$3 billion. These nutrients are not being replaced. Total fertiliser input in sub-Saharan Africa is just 9 kg per hectare, compared with 100 kg in South Asia, 135 in East and South-east Asia, 73 in Latin America and 206 in the industrialised countries. The CAADP calls for an integrated approach that combines a much greater use of organic matter and mineral fertilisers, higher-yielding hybrid seeds, smallholder irrigation and other methods. Government agricultural policies also have been poor, providing only weak economic incentives to rural producers. Privatisation and other structural adjustment policies led to an 'over-hasty withdrawal' of the state from direct production. In the absence of a sound private sector, this caused 'severe dislocation of production, farm trade and farmer support services'. Agriculture also has been starved of investment. Many African governments devote less than 1 per cent of their budgets to agriculture.

In Malawi in 2005, almost 5 million of Malawi's 13 million people were in need of emergency food aid; by 2007, because of affordable fertilisers, the country produced a maize surplus of over one million tonnes thanks, in large part, to a new fertiliser and seed subsidy sponsored by the Malawian government, with help from the UK Department for International Development (DFID). The extra production in 2007 was valued at $100–$160 million, far exceeding the $70 million cost of the seed and fertiliser subsidy.

Investment in agricultural research

Public investment in agricultural research is of particular importance for achieving food security in developing countries. The private sector is unlikely to undertake much of the research needed by small farmers because it cannot expect sufficient returns. IFPRI research has shown that the annual rates of return to agricultural research and development are, on average, 73 per cent. Despite this evidence, low-income developing countries grossly under-invest in agricultural research: less than 0.5 per cent of the value of their agricultural production, compared to 2 per cent in higher-income countries. Sub-Saharan Africa, which desperately needs productivity increases in agriculture, has only 42 agricultural researchers per million economically active persons in agriculture, compared with 2,458 in industrial countries. Efforts to improve longer-term productivity on smallholder farms, with an emphasis on staple food crops, must be accelerated. Research and policies are also needed to help farmers, communities and governments to cope better with risks resulting from such factors as poor market integration, poorly functioning markets and climatic fluctuations. More research must be directed to the development of appropriate technologies for the sustainable intensification of agriculture in resource-poor areas, where a high percentage of poor people live, and where environmental risks are severe. The needed research must join all appropriate scientific tools together, with better use of the insights of traditional indigenous knowledge. Research and technology alone will not drive agricultural growth. The full beneficial effects of agricultural research and technological change will materialise only if government policies are conducive to, and supportive of, poverty alleviation and sustainable management of natural resources.

Research shows that a 1 per cent increase in agricultural yields decreases the percentage of population living on less than US$1 a day by 0.64 to 0.91 per cent, with a slightly higher reduction in Africa. According to the World Bank, a 10 per cent increase in crop yields leads to a 9 per cent decrease in the percentage of people living on less than US$1 a day. The same effect is not achieved by growth in the manufacturing and service sectors.

Research has shown that improved varieties of millet, sorghum and other traditional African grains can also significantly boost yields. Beyond seeds, farmers need access to animal health care, safe pesticides and other inputs, as well as training in agro-forestry and other skills. Africa's agricultural research institutes and extension services have very little capacity to engage in new scientific research or get existing technologies out into farmers' fields. In part, such problems can be overcome by finding new ways to generate and handle scientific knowledge, says the CAADP. Farmers themselves should be more closely involved in both research and dissemination.

Market access for smallholder farmers

Investment in market access is import because as smallholder farmers increase agricultural production there is a need to market their outputs. Without efficient marketing systems in place the gains of increased production will be eroded. Therefore there is a need for African governments to invest in good roads to facilitate market access. They also need to invest in efficient communication systems, information technology and access to credit and financial services. Once the basic conditions are in place, the uptake of productivity-increasing technologies is, however, likely to be limited to farm households that have better access to seasonal finance and to input and output markets.

External markets also are vital for Africa's producers of cotton, cocoa, coffee, tea and other export crops. Yet world market conditions have not been favourable to African farmers. Not only are international agricultural prices volatile, but African exports face restrictions on access to northern markets and are severely hurt by the high subsidies paid to rich farmers in the industrialised countries. The private sector needs government support to build capacity. In 2003, for example, Uganda could not export cereals and legumes to other countries in eastern and southern Africa, even when there was a food deficit in those countries. To address this, the Ugandan government supported a consortium of private companies by providing warehouse facilities and access to working capital. Government support together with appropriate policies – involving and encouraging private sector participation in market development – can help smallholder farmers access domestic and global markets.

While most other regions have derived significant benefits from the growth in trade and investment, which has fuelled their structural transformation, Africa has been marginalised, as its share of world trade, investment, and output has declined to negligible proportions. Policies that restrict access to the markets of developed economies have adversely affected smallholders, preventing them from fully exploiting these market opportunities. Debates surrounding biotechnology, biosafety, the World Trade Organisation and non-market barrier issues remain a puzzle to many smallholders, who require increased capacity and income to actively participate in these markets. The global economy's potential benefits can only be fully realised when the necessary complementary policies and institutions have been put in place by the respective governments. African governments need to implement sound macroeconomic fundamentals and accelerate structural reforms to make their economies less vulnerable to vacillating investor sentiments and capital flows. Africa's growth prospects and its full integration into the global economy are dependent on its domestic policies, as well as developments at the international level. Contract farming is an approach that can contribute to both increased income for farmers and higher profitability for sponsors. When efficiently organised and managed, contract farming reduces risk and uncertainty for both parties. This approach would appear to have considerable potential in countries where smallholder agriculture continues to be widespread. In many cases smallholder farmers can no longer be competitive without access to the services provided by contract farming companies.

In Madagascar, thanks to a US$17.7 million MCC investment in the Agricultural Business Investment Project, farmers have seen increased production and access to markets and, thus, increased incomes. Six Agricultural Business Centres help farmers to identify markets, form associations that help them to meet greater demands, and provide technical assistance to tackle challenges such as post-harvest storage. In 2007, one cooperative in the Menabe region produced 600 tonnes of lima beans which, when exported to Mauritius, brought in an increased net income of US$200,000 which was distributed throughout the value chain. The 78 farmers of the producing cooperative each earned US$940, $300 above the average household income in the region.

Investment in education

The development of rural education is vital to the success of rural development and sustainable livelihoods. There is need for more, better schools close to rural communities, and quality teaching staff need to be properly remunerated. Different education systems should be introduced to ensure that land reform programmes succeed. Diploma courses in agriculture could equip future land reform beneficiaries with the relevant skills, while short courses in agriculture could build the capacity of rural farmers, and equip them with modern farming methods. Skills development programmes to provide the rural population with skills to start their own small- to medium-sized enterprises are also essential for rural development, as self-employment is core to improving rural livelihoods. Business and skills training and forming local cooperatives, such as craft cooperatives, also enhance trade opportunities for rural goods. For example, in Mpozolo (Eastern Cape) skills training by the REHAB programme increased the production and enthusiasm of local crafters, and their initiative to link with Mbashe Crafter Association resulted in increased orders of their craftwork (Pereira *et al.*, 2006). This shows that the provision of training and markets is vital to enhance the trade in rural goods in non-traditional markets, such as urban and international markets. A good road network is also important to facilitate the movement of the rural population to education centres and markets. Electricity in the rural schools will also enable students to have access to modern teaching facilities and learning tools, such as computers.

Investment in rural infrastructure

Smallholder farmers will not have much incentive to increase production without roads, storage facilities and the infrastructure to market their crops. The CAADP urges that more than half of the investments projected under their plan be directed toward rural infrastructure (not counting irrigation systems). In addition to roads and other 'hard' infrastructure, the CAADP argues, farmers also need 'soft' infrastructure: communications and accurate price and market information in order to take the best advantage of changing market opportunities.

In Burkina Faso, 80 per cent of the population lives in rural areas and farm activities accounted for 31 per cent of GDP in 2004. The World Bank's International Development Association (IDA) has financed irrigation schemes in rural communities and invested in infrastructure such as roads and cold-storage facilities at airports. Rural farmers are now able to irrigate their land in the dry season, and grow high-value export crops such as tomatoes and onions. In approximately 3,000 villages, the amount of irrigated land has doubled, and household incomes in the villages have increased by 30 per cent.

The rural locality of Tonka, in northern Mali, is an example of the endeavours that villagers in Africa are already making, despite extremely adverse conditions. By digging simple irrigation canals from a local river and lake, Tonka's 4,500 producers, organised in village cooperatives, have been able to increase their output of rice, millet, sorghum, potatoes, cassava, beans and other foods. Tonka's marketplaces now attract buyers from other regions in Mali, and even from across the border in neighbouring Mauritania. Thanks to the additional incomes over the past four years, Tonka's residents have been able to help finance the construction of nine primary schools, four health clinics, several wells, two livestock markets, a warehouse and several sanitation facilities.

Rural safety net

The government of South Africa also provides important social security systems in the form of non-contributory old-age pensions and child grants. These have become important sources of income for a significant number of poor and rural households. The income received from social grants is shared, reducing the possibility of some households living in abject poverty. In addition, the income is used to support informal income-generating activities, such as a trade in rural goods (such as traditional crafts) and petty trading.

Although growth benefits many of the poor, it clearly does not benefit all. Safety nets are still needed, and the rural poor in most countries are greatly disadvantaged relative to their urban counterparts when it comes to social assistance. Few developing countries include rural people in social security programmes, and the prevalence of self-employment means that unemployment compensation is largely irrelevant to those without work. South Africa is an exception in this regard, in the sense that many of the key programmes of social assistance extend to rural people and have served to prevent much hardship. In order to ensure that a safety net is sustained for the vulnerable groups, the outreach capacity of the social service departments co-coordinated by the Department of Social Development will need to be enhanced. Government should strike a balance between taking advantage of economic potential and attending to those who are vulnerable and in need of care.

Conclusions and summary

Agriculture's role in the economic development of a country changes as the transformation proceeds. In the early stages, agricultural growth, led by food staples and small farms, is a major engine of economic growth and can play a very significant role in reducing poverty. As a country develops, the agricultural sector begins to take a secondary role as an engine of growth, and the composition of its output and farm size changes. Labour migrates from agriculture, farms get larger, and higher-value foods become more important in the national diet and in production. Globalisation and trade liberalisation have weakened these traditional patterns of development to some extent, but there is little theory or evidence to suggest that today's low-income countries, especially in Africa, can bypass the need for an agricultural revolution to successfully launch their economic transformations. Within this context, small farm development offers an efficient and pro-poor option for agricultural development during the early stages of the economic transformation. However, small farms are seriously challenged today in ways that make their future precarious. Marketing chains are changing and are becoming more integrated and more demanding of quality and food safety. This is creating new opportunities for higher-value production for farmers who can compete and link to such markets, but for many the risk is that they will simply be left behind. In developing countries, small farmers also face unfair competition from rich-country farmers in many of their export and domestic markets, and they no longer have adequate support in terms of basic services and farm inputs. The spread of HIV/AIDS is further eroding the number of productive farm workers and leaving many children orphaned with limited knowledge about how to farm. Left to themselves, these forces will curtail opportunities for small farms, overly favour large farms, and lead to a premature and rapid exit of many small farmers. If most small farmers are to have a viable future, there is need for a concerted effort by governments, non-governmental organisations, and the private sector to create a more equitable and enabling economic environment for their development. This must include assistance to form effective marketing organisations, targeted agricultural research and extension, the revamping of financial systems to meet small farm credit needs, improved risk-management policies, tenure security and efficient land markets and, where all else fails, targeted safety net programmes. In addition, the public sector needs to invest in the provision of basic infrastructure, health, education and other human capital to improve market access and to increase the range of non-farm opportunities available to small farm households, including permanent migration to urban areas. These interventions are possible and could unleash significant benefits in the form of pro-poor agricultural growth. The associated public investments could also more than pay for themselves in terms of their economic and social returns. Despite the lack of financial resources of most governments in sub-Sahara Africa, the need to invest in smallholder farmers is becoming a priority, as populations are on the increase and there is a need to produce more food so as to alleviate poverty and hunger.

References

Ajayi, (2003). *Globalisation and Equity in Sub-Saharan Africa*. University of Ibadan. Ibadan, Nigeria.

Adams, M., Ashworth, V. & Raikes, P. (1993). Agricultural supporting services for land reform. Proceedings of the Land Redistribution Options Conference. Johannesburg: Land and Agriculture Policy Centre.

Ainslie, A., Kepe, T., Cinderby, S. & Petse, T. (1996). *Rural livelihoods and local level management of natural resources in the Peddie district*. Working Paper No. 42. Johannesburg: Land and Agriculture Policy Centre.

Ashley, C. & LaFrannchi, C. (1997). Livelihood strategies of rural households in Caprivi: Implications for conservancies and natural resource management. Research Discussion Paper No. 20. Windhoek: Department of Environmental Affairs.

Chen, S. & Ravallion, M. (2004). *How have the world's poorest fared since the early 1980s?* World Bank Policy Research Working Paper No. 3341. Washington, DC: World Bank.

Chen, S. & Ravallion, M. (2004). *World Development Indicators*. Washington, DC: World Bank.

Collier, P. (1997). Globalisation: Implications for Africa. Paper presented at the IMF-AERC Seminar on Trade Reforms and Regional Integration in Africa, Washington, DC (1–3 December).

Dunstan, S. (2001). Will they survive? Prospects for small farmers in sub-Saharan Africa.

Kinsey, B. (1998). Allowing land reform to work in southern Africa: A long-term perspective on rural restructuring in Zimbabwe. Paper presented to the International Conference on Land Tenure, Cape Town: University of Cape Town (January). Accessed 17 June 2009.

Kirsten, J.F. (1994). Agricultural support programmemes in the developing areas of South Africa. PhD thesis. Pretoria: University of Pretoria.

Moyo, S. (1995). *The Land Question in Zimbabwe*. Harare: SAPES Books.

NEPAD & CAADP (2008). Investment in African Agriculture and Agriculture as an Engine for Growth.

Shackleton, C.M. (1993a). Are the communal lands in need of saving? *Development Southern Africa* 10: 65–78.

Shackleton, S.E., Stadler, J.J., Jeenes, K.A., Pollard, S.R. & Gear, J.S.S. (1995). Adaptive strategies of the poor in arid and semi-arid lands – in search of sustainable livelihoods: A case study of the Bushbuckridge District, Eastern Transvaal, South Africa. Unpublished report produced for the International Institute for Environment and Development, Canada. Klaserie: Wits Rural Facility.

Shackleton, S.E., Von Maltitz, G. & Evans, J. (1998b). *Factors, conditions and criteria for the successful management of natural resources held under a common property regime: A South African perspective.* Programme for Land and Agrarian Studies, Occasional Paper No. 8. Cape Town: University of the Western Cape.

World Bank (2004). *World Development Indicators.* Washington, DC: The World Bank.

Trends and impact of investments on smallholder agriculture in Malawi

Prince Kapondamgaga and Mphatso Dakamau

Introduction

Agriculture remains the linchpin of most national economies in Africa. Therefore, most African countries have set agriculture and food security as a key priority in their development policy agenda over the past forty years. For example, the African heads of state committed at least 10 per cent of their national budgets to agriculture in the 2002 Maputo Declaration. The Comprehensive Africa Agricultural Development Programme (CAADP) states that agriculture should grow by an average of 6 per cent per annum by 2015. Despite these commitments, only 19 per cent of African nations were allocating at least 10 per cent of the national budget to agriculture by the year 2008.

Malawi has recently broken the ranks of the mismatch between rhetoric on one hand, and the reality of rural poverty and public investment in agriculture on the other hand, by implementing the 2002 Maputo Declaration. Despite registering an impressive record of budgetary allocation to agriculture in Malawi, there has been fragmented documentation of this. This chapter attempts to paint a consolidated picture of the process by:

- assessing the trends and the impact of public investment in smallholder agriculture in Malawi;
- identifying factors that have contributed to the levels of budget allocation in Malawi;
- discussing the strategies that can be used to ensure that government targets smallholder farmers sufficiently for them to benefit fully from these investments.

Background to agriculture in Malawi

Malawi's agricultural sector is dualistic in nature and comprises smallholder and large-scale farming. More than three million farm families are classified as smallholder farmers, and are mostly subsistence-oriented. Smallholder farmers produce crops such as maize, groundnuts, cassava and cotton. Smallholder agriculture accounts for 80 per cent of the country's food production, 10 per cent of the export earnings and 90 per cent of the agricultural workforce. The average smallholding is less than 1 ha (Kachule, 2004).

The estate sub-sector takes up 13 per cent of the total land area in Malawi under leasehold or freehold land tenure system. Historically, this was developed to produce cash crops such as tobacco, tea and sugar (Ministry of Agriculture & Irrigation, 1999). In the 1970s and 1980s, the estate sector expanded very quickly due to factors such as access to low-cost financing from the commercial banks; the prohibition of burley tobacco growing on customary land; duty-free access for estate products into European markets and increased demand for estate produce such as tobacco (Safalaoh, 2007).

Evolution of agriculture in independent Malawi

Malawi's agricultural sector has gone through three major phases, which were influenced by a set of domestic and international development policy shifts. The first phase was the Growth and Prosperity phase: from the early 1960s when Malawi got its independence to the late 1970s, the country witnessed remarkable growth and structural transformation. Nominal gross domestic product (GDP) grew at an average rate of 6 per cent per annum (Ministry of Economic Planning & Development, 2006). The smallholder sub-sector of agriculture achieved an average growth of 5.1 per cent per annum from 1960 to 1970 (Safaloah *et al.*, 2007). The growth was driven by 'favourable' agriculture policies, which included price controls, input subsidies,

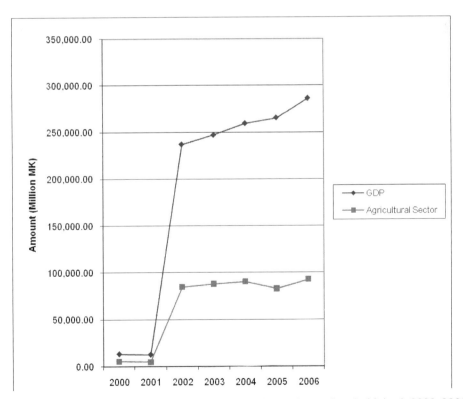

Figure 2.1 Relationship of agriculture to gross domestic product in Malawi, 2000–2006 MK (millions)

Source: National Accounts.

access to credit, a vibrant extension system and, in 1971, the establishment of a reliable market through the Agricultural Development and Marketing Corporation (ADMARC). Malawi had not yet embarked on the International Monetary Fund (IMF)/World Bank-led economic reform programmes during this phase.

The second phase was the Reform period (1980–1994). During this phase, the Malawian government adopted and started to implement the IMF/World Bank-sponsored Structural Adjustment Programmes (SAPs) which were geared at removing structural and other constraints. Key elements of SAPs were:

- the restructuring of parastatals;
- flexible management of exchange rates;
- removal of distortions (such as price controls and subsidies);
- improved resource mobilisation and expenditure allocation in the public sector;
- introduction of a multi-channel marketing system for most agricultural commodities other than those effective during the prosperity phase (Safaloah, 2007).

In spite of their sound economic sense, SAPs were a recipe for disaster in the agricultural sector, and in the economy in general. During the implementation of SAPs the agricultural sector declined to 2 per cent during most years. Different researchers such as Chinsinga (2007) have attributed the decline in agricultural growth to two primary factors. Firstly, there were sectoral structural constraints: poor infra-

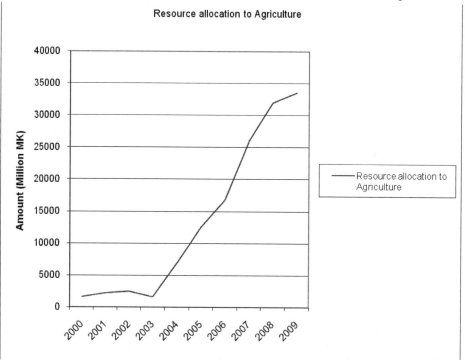

Figure: 2.2: Levels of public resource allocation to agriculture between 2000 and 2009.
Source: National Accounts

structure, unfavourable weather conditions, a high reliance on rain-fed agriculture and weak intra- and inter-sectoral linkages. Secondly, the removal of input subsidies and the dissolution of the government administered Smallholder Agricultural Credit Administration constrained the availability of inputs. The private sector did not fill the gap created by the dissolution of the government-led structures in input distribution and credit administration.

The last phase is the Post-Reform Period or the Recovery Period (1995–2009). The reform phase acted as a catalyst for the development of a number of agricultural policies and programmes because it was recognised that the prevailing policies were not adequately addressing the plight of the local people. Some sector-specific policies included the Agriculture and Livestock Development Strategy and Action Plan (ALDSAP) (1995) and the Malawi Agricultural Sector Investment Process (MASIP) (1999). The grand policy initiatives included the Poverty Alleviation Programme (1995), Vision 2020 (1998), Malawi Poverty Reduction Strategy (MPRS) (2001) and the Malawi Growth and Development Strategy (MGDS) (2005).

Also, the Malawian government introduced safety-net programmes aimed at reducing the vulnerability of communities and the promotion of rural productivity

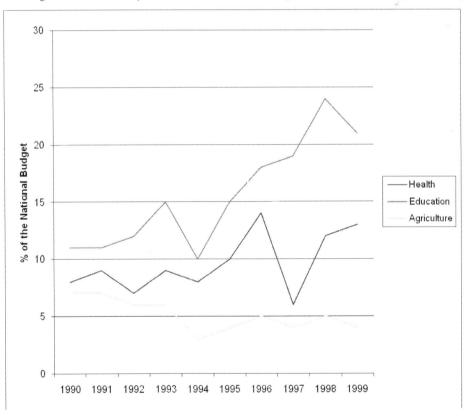

Figure 2.3:   Comparison of percentage of total national budget allocated to ministries of health, education and agriculture, 1990–1999.

Source: Ministry of Finance, 2004

through the provision of agricultural inputs. Such programmes included the Starter Pack Initiative (1998/99–1999/2000, the Targeted Input Programme (TIP) (2001/02 –2004/05) and the Farm Input Subsidy Programme (2004/05 to date).

The importance of agriculture in Malawi

Agriculture is an important sector in the economy of Malawi. It contributes 36 per cent to the total GDP, over 90 per cent of forex and 80 per cent of rural employ-ment (Ministry of Finance, 2009). The significance of the agricultural sector in the national economy is clear when one observes the relationship between develop-ments in the sector and those of the national economy. There is a close relationship between agricultural GDP and the national GDP in Malawi. For instance, when agricultural GDP registered a 25.1 per cent decline in 1992, the national economy also fell by 7.9 per cent. In 1995, when the agricultural sector was recovering from the 1994 drought as evidenced by a 39.6 per cent growth, the national GDP regis-tered a historic growth of 14.6 per cent (Ministry of Finance, 2004). Similar trends continue to be observed between GDP and the agricultural sector. Actual agricul-tural output and GDP are closely related, as seen in Figure 2.1.

The budget process in Malawi

The Ministry of Finance through other ministries is responsible for drawing up the national budget. During the budget preparation, the Ministry of Finance con-sults different stakeholders, which include the public sector, private sector, donor community and civil society organisations (CSOs). After preparation the budget is presented in Parliament for debate by and approval of the Members of Parliament (MPs). In Parliament, MPs make sure that the finance allocated to specific budget lines (called votes) is reasonable. As the budget is being debated in Parliament, the public and the CSOs present their budget analyses to the MPs, highlighting pri-orities and shortcomings, before a final decision is made. Finally, MPs go through the national budget vote by vote. Sometimes, votes are returned to the Minister of Finance for further consideration. Finally, the budget is passed.

Trends in public investments in agriculture

Agriculture has attracted a lot of attention in Malawi over the past five years. Public resources allocated to agriculture have increased annually since 2003, as shown by Figure 2.2. This is due to the government's commitment to invest more in agri-culture through the Farm Input Subsidy Programme, which was re-introduced in 2004 without compromising funding for other programmes within the agricultural sector.

Agricultural budget in relation to the national budget

The budgetary allocation to agriculture declined for the decade between 1990 and 1999, as shown in Figure 2.3. This decline in budgetary allocations is explained by the change of priorities on the side of both donors and the government. Donors reduced their support to agriculture and instead directed their resources to social sectors such as health and education, as shown in Figure 2.3. Further, 1993 represents a special case where the budget allocation was reduced to a record of 3 per cent because the subsidy on farm inputs in Malawi was removed completely as a result of the government's Structural Adjustment Programmes.

Nonetheless, expenditure on agriculture has been increasing since 2000 and reached a record high of 14 per cent in 2007, as shown in Figure 2.4. Allocations to the Ministry of Agriculture and Food Security alone form a large part of the Malawi Growth and Development Strategy (MGDS), which gets a bigger share of the national budget (62 per cent of the 2009/10 national budget). In 2009/10 the allocations for the Ministry of Agriculture and Food Security constituted 39 per cent of the total budget for MGDS-related activities, which were 13 per cent of the national budget.

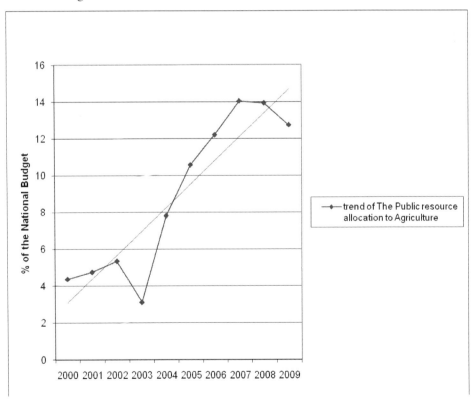

Figure 2.4: Agricultural budget as a percentage of the national budget, 2000–2009

Source: National Budget Documents, 2000–2009

Malawi's government beat the target set by the Maputo Declaration for the fifth successive year in 2009/10, as shown in Figure 2.5. The increase in the budget allocation to agriculture can be attributed to the re-introduction of subsidies for farm inputs in 2004.

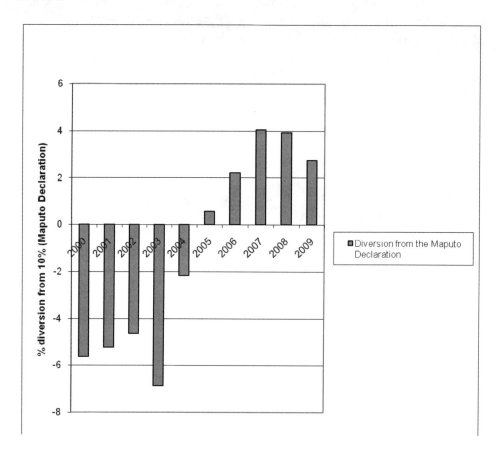

Figure 2.5:   Gap between agriculture's share in Malawi's national budget and the Maputo Declaration budget allocation to agriculture target, 2000–2009

Source: National Budget Documents, 2000–2009

Effectiveness of the budget allocation to agriculture

The immediate effect of the increase in the budgetary allocations to agriculture was an increase in crop and livestock production. Malawi was able to produce enough staple food crops, as well as 1.3 metric tonnes of surplus maize, in the 2008/09 season, a fourth surplus since the introduction of the farm input subsidy programme. Some of the surplus maize (80,000 metric tonnes) was to be exported to Kenya and Zimbabwe in 2009 by the Grain Traders and Processors Association. Also, some of the surplus maize was donated to the Republic of Swaziland and Zimbabwe in 2008.

Further, farmland productivity of several crops has improved over the years, as shown in Figure 2.6. For example, maize productivity has increased from 809 kg/ha in 2004 to above 1,650 kg/ha in 2007. This is largely due to the increased use of inputs by farmers.

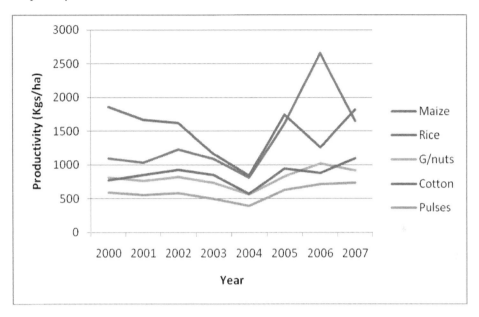

Figure 2.6: Farmland productivity for selective crops, 2000–2007
Source: Ministry of Agriculture and Food Security: Annual Statistical Bulletin, 2008

Since Malawi increased its budgetary allocation to agriculture, this sector has grown. In 2008, real growth in this sector was 11.3 per cent, which is almost twice the CAADP mark. This in turn has led to growth in other sectors of the economy because of the forward and backward linkages. For example, the manufacturing sector grew by 12.2 per cent in 2008 as a result of tobacco processing; the wholesale and retail sector grew by 8.2 per cent due to the increase in disposable income from crop sales, and the transport sector grew by 5.4 per cent because of an increase in produce (Ministry of Development Planning, 2009).

The overall effect was the growth of the economy in general. Malawi has attained a growth rate of above 7 per cent of GDP in the past three years, and the expected rate of growth in 2009 was 7.9 per cent (Ministry of Development Planning, 2009). The combined effect of the performance of the agricultural and other sectors has had a positive influence on macro human development indicators: for example, the poverty rate fell from 52 per cent in 2004 to 40 per cent in 2008, as shown in Table 2.1.

Table 2.1: Comparison of selective/key human development indicators for Malawi, 1990–2009

Description	Statistic	Year	Statistic	Year
Poverty (Head Count Index)	52%	2004	40%	2007
Enrolment in primary schools ('000s)	3 201	2005	3,307	2007
Maternal mortality ratio (per 100,000 live births)	1,120	2000	807	2006
Infant mortality rate (per 1,000 live births)	104	1992	89	2009
HIV prevalence rate	14.1%	2004	11.9%	2008

Source: Government Documents data (various years)

Factors that have contributed to the increase in the budget allocation to agriculture in Malawi

The increase in the budgetary allocation to agriculture in Malawi could be attributed to three factors: political will, advocacy and the budget preparation process.

Political will

The government that took over in 2004 has put much emphasis on agriculture. Agriculture is one of the nine priorities in the MGDS. The government re-introduced the subsidy on farm inputs in 2004 (it was scrapped in 1993 as part of the Structural Adjustment Programmes). This was a difficult decision since donors were not supportive of the initiative because they believed that doing so could distort the operations of the market. The Malawian government, under the leadership of President Bingu wa Mutharika, went ahead and financed the programme using local resources, against the wishes of the donors and the international community in the first year. As a result of the successes of the input subsidy programme in 2005, the donor community contributed finance to the programme in the subsequent years. The Malawian government also took the lead in financing the development budget of the agriculture sector, as shown in Figure 2.7.

Advocacy

The role of advocacy cannot be overemphasised in the recent increase in the budgetary allocation to agriculture in Malawi. Most of the CSOs pursue several methods of advocacy in an effort to influence the government to increase the budgetary allocation to agriculture. The roles of three CSOs are discussed in the sections that follow.

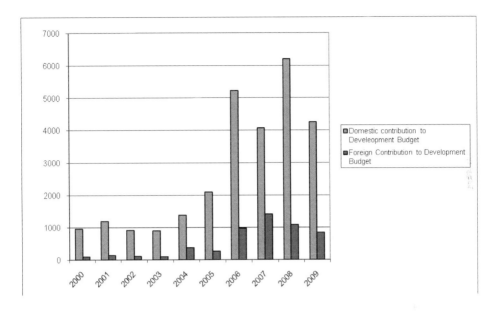

Figure 2.7: Donor and domestic resource contribution to development budget of the Ministry of Agriculture

Source: National Budget Documents, 2000–2009

The Malawi Economic Justice Network (MEJN)

The Malawi Economic Justice Network (MEJN) analyses the national budget when it has been pronounced in Parliament each year. The main objective for the analysis is to crosscheck the extent to which Priority Poverty Expenditures (PPEs) have been given the desired priority In the budget, while making corresponding cuts in expenditure on non-priority areas.

The budget analyses are done at two levels. The first is done soon after the Minister of Finance has presented the budget to Parliament. This level is intended to establish trends and identify general issues, changes and developments without delving deeply into the figures. This results in a report that is made available to MPs so that they are guided in their debate on the budget. Members of civil society and the media are also furnished with the reports so that they can use their own established channels to lobby and advocate to the MPs as the debate goes on.

The second level is the preparation of a comprehensive analysis report. The figures are scrutinised to establish any changes or trends. Any new policies introduced are also analysed in terms of their possible impact on the poor. The Comprehensive Budget Analysis is also made available to MPs, government, donors and the rest of civil society.

Civil Society Agricultural Network

Civil Society Agriculture Network (CISANET) has also been involved in the budget tracking surveys to provide evidence from the community (smallholder farmers) on how the Ministry of Agriculture has delivered, based on the resources provided by the public budget. The findings of such studies are presented to the Parliamentary Committee of Agriculture and the Budgets and Finance Committees, amongst others. The presentation and use of these findings are presented and used during the pre-budget and post-budget sessions.

Farmers' Union of Malawi

The Farmers' Union of Malawi, which comprises over 200,000 smallholder farmers, also monitors specific programmes, such as the Farm Input Subsidy Programme. For instance, it monitors whether the intended beneficiaries of the programme do get the inputs.

Ways of making government accountable for the expenditure on agriculture

Monitoring and evaluation (M&E) should be promoted at all levels to make sure that governments rightly target the smallholder farmers and that the planned public resources are properly accounted for. In cognisance of this fact, MEJN and CISANET carry out budget monitoring studies. These include *Service Delivery Satisfaction Surveys* and *Budget Tracking*. Such studies are meant to measure the level of satisfaction (or dissatisfaction) of Malawian citizens with the agricultural services provided by government. The monitoring exercise of the Farm Input Subsidy Programme by the Farmers' Union of Malawi helps to identify issues of targeting and tracking to monitor whether the 'right people' are benefiting from the programme. It is worth noting that these monitoring and evaluation studies are being used by government in Malawi – the effectiveness of such a programme will always depend on the receptiveness of government to listen to the different stakeholders in the economy.

Monitoring and evaluation programmes lack adequate resources, however. Most CSOs rely on grants for their operations, so sustainability of such monitoring exercises may be compromised. Governments should also strengthen their own monitoring and evaluation systems. The government of Malawi has strengthened its M&E to such an extent that almost all the ministries have their own M&E officers. M&E by government can run concurrently with that being done by the CSOs, as is the case in Malawi.

The effectiveness of M&E depends on the designing of the projects and programmes to a great extent. One monitors and evaluates based on some clearly stated objectives and targets. It would also be important that the national budget should be framed in such a way that it will facilitate the M&E exercise. The national budget of Malawi is an output-based budget. For instance, the Ministry of Agriculture and

Food Security comes up with targets and corresponding activities and budget to meet those targets. This facilitates M&E when assessing the performance of the ministry as a whole or specific programmes.

Conclusion

In conclusion, the budget allocation to agriculture has increased since 2003 in Malawi. Specifically, more resources are allocated to the Farm Input Subsidy Programme, which has been successfully implemented without causing a decline in other programmes. Through increased spending on agriculture, Malawi has achieved growth in the agricultural sector, which has resulted in food security and poverty alleviation, and growth of the entire economy. This achievement came about because of political will and the role of advocacy institutions.

M&E is vital for targeting and ensuring that farmers get the most from government budgetary allocation, and should be done by CSOs as well as government. Clear pre-determined targets in the national budget should facilitate the M&E exercise.

References

Chinsinga, B. (2007). *The Fall and Rise of Agriculture? Reflections and Debates about the Future of Agriculture in Malawi.* Available on: www.future-agricultures.org/pdf%20files/EEA_Malawi.ppt.

Kachule, R. (2004). *Rural Producer Organisations and Policy Formulation in Malawi.* Available on: www.nibr.no/content/download/2407/10106/file/2004-127.pdf.

Ministry of Agriculture & Food Security. (2007). Annual Statistical Bulletin. Malawi.

Ministry of Agriculture & Irrigation. (1999). Review of Malawi agricultural policies and strategies. Draft main report.

Ministry of Development Planning & Cooperation. (2009). Annual Economic Report. Malawi.

Ministry of Economic Planning & Development, (2006). Annual Economic Report. Malawi.

Ministry of Finance. (2009). Financial statement for the 2009/2010 national budget. Malawi.

Ministry of Finance. (2004). Agricultural Sector Analysis. Malawi.

Ministry of Finance. (2000–2009). National Budget Document. Malawi.

Ministry of Natural Resources & Environmental Affairs. (2004). Malawi National Strategy for Sustainable Development. Lilongwe.

Safalaoh. A. *et al.* (2007). The maize ASTI system: Lessons from a national ASTI: Case study in Malawi Malawi: Bunda College of Agriculture.

Chapter 3

Trends in public expenditure and its implications for agriculture in Tanzania

DAMIAN M. GABAGAMBI

Introduction

Tanzania, like many other African countries is an agrarian economy with agriculture accounting for close to one-third of the GDP (Bank of Tanzania, 2009). However, like many developing countries of Africa, Tanzania's agriculture is undercapitalised, uncompetitive and underperforming, and is characterised by relatively low yields, overdependence on primary exports and high price volatility (Hazell *et al.*, 2003). This partly explains the low sector growth, which averaged 4.4 per cent in the period 2000 to 2008. Consequently the economic situation of the people deriving their livelihood from agriculture has continued to deteriorate.

Conscious of the need to stimulate the stagnant situation in agriculture and to prioritise the sector in order to harness its full potential so as to guarantee sustainable food security and ensure economic prosperity for her people, Tanzania embarked on implementing the Maputo Declaration through the Agricultural Sector Development Programme (ASDP). The Maputo Declaration is a road map for capitalising agriculture on the continent with the objective of ensuring that this sector receives at least 10 per cent of the respective countries' national budgets. This would in turn make the sector attain a 6 per cent growth rate and cut hunger in half by 2015 (Mukuti & Barasa, 2008). But since the decision to increase the budgetary allocation and endorse the Comprehensive Africa Agricultural Development Programme (CAADP), it is doubtful whether Tanzania's expenditure on agriculture is in line with the CAADP target.

This chapter examines the Tanzanian government's commitment to increasing its budgetary allocation to agriculture, and whether such funds have been effective in reaching resource-poor farmers and reducing poverty. Ultimately, policy reforms that could bring about anticipated rural transformation are proposed. This chapter comprises four parts. The first part examines commitment at policy level, which is fundamental for policy interventions. The aim is to show whether policy objectives are clearly aimed at addressing the challenges facing the poor in the agricultural sector. The second part explores the trends in public expenditure to see whether spending on agriculture in Tanzania reflects the government's commitment to CAADP targets. Part three demonstrates the current situation of poverty incidence amid efforts to improve the livelihood of the poor. The fourth part examines the efficiency in spending the funds allocated to agriculture to see whether the resources are reaching targeted beneficiaries.

Agricultural policies and the interests of smallholder farmers in Tanzania

In an endeavour to transform the livelihood of the rural people and agriculture in general, Tanzania developed a chain of strategy documents and policy initiatives embedded in the Tanzania Development Vision 2025 and the National Strategy for Growth and Reduction of Poverty (NSGRP), colloquially called MKUKUTA (Matee & Shem, 2005). A list of some of these initiatives is presented in Appendix 3A. Suffice it to say that critical examination reveals that smallholder farmers are at the centre of the objectives of the national development vision and all the policies, strategies, programmes and projects. Statements such as ensuring food self-sufficiency and food security, reducing income poverty, improving standards of living in the rural area, supplying raw materials, improving production and productivity, improving marketing and processing technologies characterise policy and strategy documents. The subsequent sections describe objectives of selected policies, namely, MKUKUTA, the Agricultural Sector Development Programme (ASDP) and Agricultural Marketing Systems Development Programme (AMSDP).

Strategy for Growth and Reduction of Poverty (NSGRP or MKUKUTA)

The NSGRP for Tanzania was set out with very detailed goals for the period 2005 to 2010. The strategy was set up in three clusters, each with main goals, pinned out with targets and means to reach them. The cluster that is relevant to this chapter is Cluster I which covers issues related to growth and reduction of income poverty. Cluster I has six goals, namely, ensuring sound economic management; promoting sustainable and broad-based growth; improving food availability and accessibility at household level in urban and rural areas; reducing income poverty of both men and women in rural areas; and reducing income poverty of both men and women in urban areas. Critical examination reveals that these objectives affect the lives of smallholder farmers in a direct way. This is because about 75 per cent of the population in Tanzania lives in rural areas, working on farms to earn their livelihood. Whether the livelihood of the farmers has improved in the reference period is a contentious issue. Phase I of MKUKUTA was concluded in 2010, and Phase II has just started.

Agricultural Sector Development Strategy

The government of Tanzania recently developed an Agricultural Sector Development Strategy (ASDS) and its operational programme, Agricultural Sector Development Programme (ASDP), the objectives of which are to achieve a sustained agricultural growth rate of 5 per cent per annum, by transforming from subsistence to commercial agriculture. The principal outcomes of the programme are expected to be higher farm productivity, profitability and incomes through improved access to and use of relevant agricultural knowledge and technology by farmers, increased district level investment and improved market development. All these outcomes are in line with anticipated transformation at farm household level in Tanzania.

Agricultural Marketing Systems Development Programme (AMSDP)

The major components of AMSDP included (i) agricultural marketing policy development, aimed at supporting the policy formulation and implementation process for the sake of improved regulatory and legislative environment pertaining to the marketing of agricultural crops at both national and local government levels; (ii) producer empowerment and market linkages to increase the benefits smallholder farmers, traders and processors gain in interacting with the market in an organised and sustainable manner; (iii) Financial Market Support Services aimed at supporting the efforts to increase the level of commercial operations in rural areas through sustainable access to credit for small and medium-size rural traders/processors and farmers; (iv) agricultural marketing infrastructure development, designed to help reduce the high marketing transaction costs associated with inadequate road infrastructure and market facilities in rural areas. Clearly, the objectives of AMSDP were focused and had a direct bearing on smallholder farmers. This programme has run its course and has been wound up. Whether there are observable impacts on the ground is a debatable issue.

Government spending in favour of the farm sector

This can be looked at from different angles: firstly, from the point of view of the amount of money allocated to the agricultural sector through the national budget, and secondly by examining specific projects and interventions implemented with the objectives of benefiting smallholder farmers.

Trends of agricultural budget in Tanzania

Since 2001/02 the agricultural budget has generally been increasing gradually. It was only 3.0 per cent of the national budget in 2000/1 and had more than doubled to 8.0 per cent in 2010/11. But statistics do not suggest that this increment is associated with the CAADP decision because the increment started the same year the Declaration was made in 2003, and dropped by 1 per cent to 4.7 per cent a year later. Two years later, in 2006/07, there was no increment at all (Table 3.1). Nevertheless, the 8.0 per cent mark is far below the 10 per cent stipulated in CAADP. However, the 10 per cent target seems to be a tough nut to crack for many other African Union member states. FAO[1] and Regional Strategic Analysis and Knowledge Support System (ReSAKSS, 2009) statistics indicate that in 2007, only eight countries had achieved the target of allocating at least 10 per cent of their national budgets to agriculture. These countries were Burkina Faso (20 per cent), Niger (15 per cent),

---

[1]   FAO data available at the AU website: www.africa-union.org

Guinea (13.5 per cent), Senegal (13 per cent), Malawi (12 per cent), Ethiopia (11 per cent), Mali (10.5 per cent) and Ghana (10 per cent). The average for the 38 countries was 6.6 per cent. Tanzania ranked twentieth in the list of 39 countries.

Table 3.1: Trend of budget allocation to agriculture in billion TSh (2001/02–2010/11)

Year	Total agric. budget	Total national budget	% increase in agric. budget	Agric. budget as % of national budget	% change in the allocation
2001/02	52.1	1,764.7		3.0	0.0
2002/03	84.5	2,219.2	62.2	3.8	0.8
2003/04	148.6	2,607.2	75.9	5.7	1.9
2004/05	157.7	3,347.5	6.1	4.7	−1.0
2005/06	233.3	4,035.1	48.0	5.8	1.1
2006/07	276.6	4,788.5	18.5	5.8	0.0
2007/08	372.4	6,000.0	34.6	6.2	0.4
2008/09	440.1	7,216.1	18.2	6.1	−0.1
2009/10	666.9	9,500.0	34.0	7.0	0.9
2010/11	903.8	11,610.0	26.2	7.8	0.8

Source: Budget volumes for respective years

Government spending on smallholder interventions in Tanzania

In specific terms, the government spends a considerable amount of money on the poor farmers. In the previous section it was stated that there is a chain of programmes and projects that are being implemented in the interest of smallholder farmers. Table 3.2 presents the duration and costs of some of these programmes, and the sources of funding.[2] The aim is to demonstrate that substantial amounts of money are apparently being spent in the interest of the poor in the farming sector. It could be noted that between 2001 and 2015 the government of Tanzania will have spent US$ 495.5 million in addressing social and economic problems at the grassroots level, benefiting more than four million smallholder farmers. Of these funds, 43.1 per cent (US$213.7 million) will be loans from different institutions.

Another angle of looking at the way in which the money from the government trickles down to smallholder farmers is to examine the subsidies to farmers for fertilisers, seeds and farm implements in order to increase food production. Between 2003/04 and 2009/10 the government spent TSh231.6 billion to subsidise various inputs for smallholder farmers.[3] In 2010/11 alone the government is to spend TSh146 billion for the same purpose (Table 3.3).

---

[2]   Extracted from project documents available at IFAD website and Ministry of Finance and Economic Affairs in Tanzania.

[3]   Ministry of Agriculture, Food Security and Cooperatives in Tanzania.

Table 3.2: Some programmes addressing smallholder farmer development issues

Programme	Duration	Total cost (million US$)	Source of fund (million US$)	Target house-holds (benefi-ciaries)
Rural Financial Services Programme (RFSP)	2001–2010	23.8	IFAD Loan (19.5); IFAD grant (0.45); OPEC (2.2); Swiss Agency for Development Cooperation (2.2)	55,000
Agricultural Marketing Systems Development Programme (AMSDP)	2002–2009	52.8	IFAD Loan (16.3); African Development Fund (AfDF) (25.0); Development Co-operation Ireland (1.1); Deficit (4.5)	25,000
Agricultural Sector Development Programme (ASDP)	2006–2013	190.1	IFAD Loan (56.0); Basket Fund (89.7 Deficit (9.2)	1,489,320
Rural Micro, Small and Medium Enterprise Support Programme	2007–2014	25.3	IFAD Loan (19.5); IFAD grant (0.45); Development coopera-tion Ireland (0.9)	23 districts
Agricultural Sector Development Programme – Livestock: Support for Pastoral and Agro-Pastoral Development (AMDP-L)	2007–2015	29.1	IFAD Loan (20.6); Belgium Survival Fund for Third World (BSF) (4.8)	460,839
Agricultural Services Support Programme (ASSP)	2000–2014	114.4	IFAD loan (25.0); Basket Fund (72.7)	549,842
Tanzania Social Action Fund (TASAF)	2000–2004	60.0	World Bank loan	40 districts
Tanzania Social Action Fund II (TASAF II)	2010–2015	35.0	World Bank loan	121 districts

Table 3.3: Some programmes to address smallholder farmer development issues

Season	Fertiliser quantity (000 tonnes)	Improved seeds (000 tonnes)	Value (billion TSh)	Subsidy as % of total agric. budget
2003/04	39.4		2.0	1.3
2004/05	81.8		7.2	4.6
2005/06	63.0		7.5	3.2
2006/07	89.9	0.8	21.0	7.6
2007/08	83.0	1.1	19.5	5.2
2008/09	155.0	6.0	71.5	16.2
2009/10	150.0	15.2	102.8	15.4
2010/11	200.0	20.0	146.0	16.2

Source: Ministry of Agriculture, Food Security and Cooperatives (MAFSC)

It can be noted that the amount of money spent on input subsidy has been increasing over time. In 2003 when the Maputo Declaration was made, the amount of the agricultural budget that went into subsidising fertiliser was a mere 1.3 per cent. Over the following five years the proportion had increased to 16.2 per cent. Despite this increase, the rate of fertiliser use is still too low to create any meaningful improvement in agricultural productivity in the country. It is estimated that Tanzania's total potential fertiliser market demand is around 680,000 tonnes per year. The annual average fertiliser subsidy is only about 10 per cent of the total fertiliser requirements of the country (Tanzania Fertiliser Company, 2006). As much as this may show commitment of the government to increase productivity within the agriculture sector, there is no reason whatsoever to believe that the subsidised fertiliser reaches the target beneficiaries – more on this later in this chapter.

In addition, statistics indicate that between 2006/07 and 2008/09), the government, through the District Agriculture Development Plans (DADPS), provided loans to farmers to buy 186 power tillers, as well as allocating significant resources to irrigation (Table 3.4).

Whether all these billions are being spent strategically to eradicate poverty among farming communities is an issue that cannot be ascertained. At least one thing is certain: the national debt is swelling and the number of people falling below the poverty line is increasing, as highlighted in the following section.

The National Strategy for Economic Growth and Poverty Reduction aimed at reducing the incidence of basic needs poverty to 24 per cent in rural areas and to 12 per cent in urban areas by 2010. The Millennium Development Goal (MDG) target is a 50 per cent reduction in the incidence of poverty between 1990 and 2015.

Table 3.4: Investment in irrigation in implementing CAADP (million TSh)

Investment	2006/07	2007/08	2008/09
District Irrigation Development Fund (DIDF)	164.0	7,386.2	4,634.8
National Irrigation Development Fund (NIDF)	1,258.8	3,197.5	3,357.4
Total	1,422.8	10,583.7	7,992.2

Source: Ministry of Agriculture, Food Security and Cooperatives in Tanzania

In 1991/92, 39 per cent of Tanzanian households were living below the basic needs poverty line; the MDG target was to reduce this proportion to 19.5 per cent by 2015. However, data from the HBS 2000/01 and 2007 show a limited decline in income poverty level over the last period in all areas (Table 3.5). Over this period, the proportion of the population below the basic needs poverty line declined slightly from 35.7 per cent to 33.6 per cent, and the incidence of food poverty fell from 18.7 per cent to 16.6 per cent. It could be noted that the fall in poverty over the period from 1991/92 to 2000/01 was larger; basic needs and food poverty level both declined by approximately three percentage points. This is clear proof that spending on agriculture does not necessarily bring about improvement in the livelihood of the poor in the farm sector.

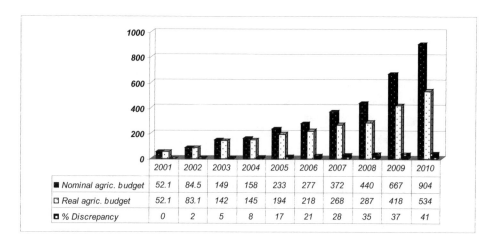

	2001	2002	2003	2004	2005	2006	2007	2008	2009	2010
■ Nominal agric. budget	52.1	84.5	149	158	233	277	372	440	667	904
☐ Real agric. budget	52.1	83.1	142	145	194	218	268	287	418	534
▣ % Discrepancy	0	2	5	8	17	21	28	35	37	41

Figure 3.1: Nominal and real budget (in billion TSh) allocated to agriculture (2001–2008/09)

Table 3.5: Incidence of poverty in Tanzania between 1991/92 and 2007

Poverty line	Year	Dar es Salaam	Other urban areas	Rural areas	Mainland Tanzania
Basic needs	1991/92	28.1	28.7	40.8	38.6
	2000/01	17.6	25.8	38.7	35.7
	2007	16.4	24.1	37.6	33.6
Food	1991/92	13.6	15.0	23.1	21.6
	2000/01	7.5	13.2	20.4	18.7
	2007	7.4	12.9	18.4	16.6

Source: HBS 2000/2001 and 2007

Effectiveness of funds allocated to agriculture

There is a general misconception that increasing budget allocation to agriculture increases funds flowing into the sector. Unfortunately this is not always the case. Whether the sector benefits or not depends on many factors, including inflation, the mismatch between allocated and disbursed funds, and corruption.

Budgetary allocations to agriculture adjusted to inflation

It was observed earlier that the budget for agriculture has generally been rising over time. But technically, these budget figures are nominal values which do not necessarily reflect a real increase in allocation because inflation is not taken into account. It is possible that actually little or no increment has taken place over the reference period. To address the problem of inflation the nominal budget values were deflated into real values by dividing nominal values by respective consumer price indices (CPIs) as shown in the formula below:

$$\textit{Real agricultural value} \quad = \quad \frac{\textit{Nominal agricultural budget value}}{\textit{National Consumer Price Index (CPI)}} \quad \textit{x 100}$$

Taking 2001 as a base year (2001=100), data from the National Bureau of Statistics (NBS)[4] indicate that the CPIs for subsequent years are 101.0 (2002), 104.5 (2003), 108.9 (2004), 120.9 (2005), 129.6 (2006), 138.8 (2007), 153.3 (2008, 159.5 (2009) and

---

[4] National Bureau of Statistics is responsible for data collection and analysis for policy use in Tanzania.

169.2 (2010).[5] The resulting real values of budget allocated to agriculture in relation to the nominal budget values are presented in Figure 3.1. It should be noted that when the influence of inflation is factored in, more insights come to light. Although the agricultural budget has been increasing tremendously over the years, in real terms the increase has been lower than reported.

As shown in Figure 3.1, the discrepancy between nominal and real budget values increased from 2 per cent in 2002 to 41 per cent in 2010. This is equivalent to a difference of up to TSh 369.6 billion. Nevertheless, examination of the percentage increase for the agricultural sector indicates that the increase does not exhibit any specific pattern; it fluctuates from one year to another, indicating that the change has no association with expenditure increase. However, the percentage change in GDP seems to follow closely the performance of the agricultural sector (Figure 3.2): the peaks and troughs on the two curves seem to coincide. The policy implication for this is that if the government formulated policies to increase and stabilise agricultural growth, the economic growth for Tanzania would be enormous.

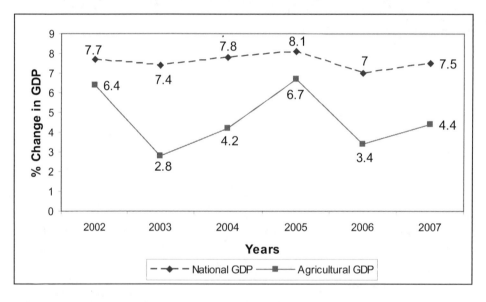

Figure 3.2: Percentage change in national GDP and agricultural GDP[6]

Mismatch between approved and actual expenditure

In the language of national budgeting three terminologies are commonly used, sometimes interchangeably. They are 'budget estimate', 'approved expenditure' and 'actual expenditure'. Budget estimates refer to the figures presented to the Parliament

---

5   The CPI figures for 2009 and 2010 were extrapolated from the time series data of the CPI for previous years because they are not yet available at NBS.
6   Constructed from BoT Economic Bulletin for the quarter ending March 2009.

for deliberations. The Parliament approves the estimates with or without alterations; these estimates become approved expenditures (Rønsholt *et al.*, 2003). But in most cases there is a mismatch between approved expenditures and the actual funds released by the treasury to the respective ministries. The actual funds released is what is referred to as the actual budget.

Data from the Appropriation Account Books of the Ministry of Agriculture, Food Security and Cooperatives between 2000/01 and 2007/08 indicate that between 2000/01 and 2009/10 the deficit between approved budget and actual expenditure ranged between 6 and 49 per cent (Table 3.6). There is no clear trend that suggests the association between the deficits and the Maputo Declaration. However, it can be observed that the deficit for recurrent budget is increasing over time. For example, in 2000/01 the deficit was only TSh0.04 billion (almost 0 per cent of the approved estimate), but in 2006/07 the deficit was recorded at TSh17.9 billion (23.5 per cent of the approved estimate). On the other hand, the deficit for the development budget in 2000/01 was TSh12.8 billion, equivalent to 81 per cent of the approved recurrent budget. But in 2006/07 the gap had lessened to 39.2 per cent (Appendix 3B). These results may suggest that either the government is placing more emphasis on development expenditure or most members of the donor community have released support to the budget, as promised, in respective years.

Table 3.6: Approved and disbursed funds for the Ministry of Agriculture

Year	Approved (TSh billion)	Disbursed (TSh billion)	Deficit	Deficit as percentage of approved
2000/01	26.1	13.3	−12.8	−49
2001/02	25.5	23.4	−2.2	−8
2002/03	34.8	30.2	−4.6	−13
2003/04	73.0	60.4	−12.6	−17
2005/06	133.5	97.4	−36.2	−27
2006/07	122.2	86.3	−35.9	−29
2007/08	131.9	124.1	−7.8	−6

Corruption elements

The funds allocated to agriculture might be spent on overhead expenditures and/or misappropriated. Cases of misspending government funds on unnecessary non-productive items such as conferences and expensive vehicles for government officials are rampant in Tanzania. In addition, corruption cases reported within the Ministry of Agriculture and other lead ministries indicate that funds allocated to agriculture do not necessarily reach the sector. For example, reports of the Controller and

Auditor General (CAG) for June 2007 indicate that funding of TSh14.5 billion was mismanaged between 2001 and 2006. This mismanagement included unauthorised expenditure, improperly vouchered or unvouchered expenditure, irregular payments, and payments not supported by pro forma invoices. Similarly, the CAG report for June 2008 indicated gross irregularities, especially in the fertiliser subsidy programme. Irregularities include receipts in cashbooks but not in bank statements – TSh129.1 million; purchase of additional assets not accounted – TSh2.0 billion; goods worth TSh9.0 million not taken on ledger charges; payment amounting to TSh36.0 million without supporting documents; the irregular procurement of furniture worth TSh60.4 million; TSh7.4 million transferred to the sub-treasury for seminars and workshops could not be traced; untraced balance of subsidised UREA fertiliser (100 metric tonnes) worth TSh20.1 million; and unreceipted subsidised fertiliser to farmers worth TSh30.3 million. For details about the audit queries related to fertiliser, see Appendices 3C and 3D.

Ineffectiveness of the Input Subsidy Programme

As stated previously, Tanzania is spending billions on fertiliser subsidies. As much as this may show commitment by the government to increase productivity in the agricultural sector, there is no reason to believe that the subsidised fertiliser reaches target beneficiaries. Constraints in the distribution system are widely documented. Six major problems are often cited: firstly, subsidised fertiliser ends up in the shops of input suppliers and gets sold at the market price; secondly, fertiliser spills to neighbouring countries; thirdly, more often than not delayed fertiliser delivery is common – this may be the reason why farmers become incentivised to sell it to traders; fifthly, re-bagging is a common practice in the warehouse before distribution to the farmers. Lastly, there is no mechanism to ensure that the fertiliser distributed is of the right quality. Furthermore, the voucher system used to allocate fertiliser to the beneficiaries is practically ineffective, for two reasons. One, there is a possibility for farmers and input traders to collude and embezzle the system by a farmer taking a few bags of fertiliser and selling the rest of the vouchers to the trader who would submit them to the government and get money. Two, the voucher system is discriminatory against the poor. Those who get fertiliser are progressive farmers who have shown demonstrable ability to produce more crops. In other words, the poor farmers, who form the majority of the rural population, are absolutely left out.

To resolve this problem, the government introduced the voucher system to ensure that the fertiliser reached target farmers. But critical examination of the system reveals that the voucher system has not solved the problem. The voucher entitles the bearer to a subsidy of about 40 per cent of the fertiliser price. Fertiliser in Tanzania, DAP for example, costs about US$ 100. Waiving 40 per cent means a farmer has to pay US$ 60 to secure a bag of fertiliser. Most farmers do not have this amount of money, so they resort to collusion with the stockists.

Budget template not pro-poor

Stakeholders would like to see the budget allocated to agriculture increased, but before that is in effect there is a need to review the current budget templates to identify areas for improvement. For example, at the moment more than 50 per cent of the development budget is spent on overhead costs (Table 3.7).

Table 3.7: Detailed development budget for MAFSC, 2007/08

S/N	Code description	Funds allocated (TSh billion)	% of total
1	Per diems	2.53	2.39
2	Diesel/petrol	1.11	1.05
3	Food and refreshment/lodging & boarding	0.99	0.93
4	Conference facilities & meetings	0.49	0.46
5	Extra duty allowance	0.05	0.05
6	Stationery/sundry supplies/printing/technical materials/utilities	0.71	0.67
7	Travel tickets/rental charges – domestic	0.58	0.55
8	Travel tickets – foreign	0.17	0.16
9	Certified seeds/fertiliser/agrochemicals/breeding stock	0.41	0.39
10	Tools and implements/car/furniture	5.51	5.19
11	Consultancy/professional fee	9.83	9.26
12	Services & repairs	1.29	1.22
13	Casual labour	0.02	0.02
14	HIV epidemics	0.01	0.01
15	Honoraria	0.14	0.14
16	Sitting allowance	0.11	0.1
17	Training – domestic & foreign	7.54	7.1
18	Advertising & publicity	0.10	0.1
19	Technical assistance	0.86	0.81
20	Salaries & remunerations for staff	1.06	1.0
21	Road & building rehabilitation/water catchments/farm structure	4.94	4.66
22	Self-help schemes	15.25	14.37
23	Project implementation in the regions	52.12	49.11
24	Miscellaneous	0.28	0.26
	TOTAL	**106.12**	**100.00**

Note: Item 23 is the money that apparently trickles down to farmers. (Source: Ministry of Agriculture (MAFSC), vote 43, 2007)

Further analysis by dropping outliers in the data (items 22 and 23) reveals that the greatest portion of the development budget is spent on consultancy and professional fees, which accounts for 25.4 per cent of the budget. This is followed by training (19.4 per cent), tools and equipment (14.2 per cent), infrastructure rehabilitation (12.4 per cent) and per diems (6.5 per cent). For details see Appendix 3E.

Tracking the funds that are allocated to regions and subsequent district and town councils is a task that requires an enormous amount of time and resources. But it can be said that the general picture resembles that at national level. The expenditure components are basically the same – salaries, travel expenses, per diems, training material, building rehabilitation, extra duty allowances, etc. To demonstrate this, we analyse expenditure for one district council, Mwanza City Council, using data collected by Agenda Participation 2000 in 2008. It was revealed that the development budget was still below 40 per cent, and more than 25 per cent of the budget was allocated to running the city treasury office. It was also noted that actual spending lagged behind the budgeted amount for all spending categories (Figure 3.3).

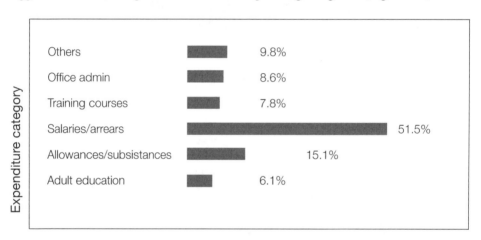

Figure 3.3: Proportion of spending for different spending categories for Mwanza City Council.

Source: Modified from Kulaba, 2009

Based on these facts, it can be argued that allocating the 10 per cent of the national budget to agriculture and rural development would not cure all the problems facing agriculture, especially in a situation where the M&E mechanism is weak or does not exist at all. For development expenditure in Tanzania, the M&E is embedded in the project or programme plans, and there are always M&E officers for each project/programme. For recurrent expenditures there are virtually no M&E mechanisms in Tanzania, apart from ordinary auditing by the Controller and Auditor General (CAG). Normally, CAG's report lags two or three years behind the expenditure. In the previous government regimes, CAG's report used to be confidential, but under the current government this report is released for public consumption.

Conclusion

Although the budget allocated to agriculture for Tanzania has been increasing over the last five years, the country has failed to reach the 10 per cent CAADP target. In 2009/10 the allocation hit the highest mark of 7.0 per cent. The funds are spent on a chain of programmes, including an input subsidy. This chapter has demonstrated that funds trickling down to the grassroots from the central government level are clear at macro level, but that the picture becomes blurred at micro level. It has also been demonstrated that despite enticing statements in policy documents, statistics indicate that smallholder farmers still face similar problems to the ones the policies promised to resolve: food insecurity is still endemic, as manifested by the banning of cross-border trade in grain; lack of water, pasture resources and proper arrangements to allocate land still results in conflicts between farmers and pastoralists in the country; and the number of people living below the poverty line is increasing. Suffice it to say that the policies and strategies have not had any significant impact on the smallholder farmers, despite the billions spent on developing and implementing them.

The analysis presented here was based on information extracted from government documents such as budgets and project material. It would be appropriate to design a survey that would collect primary information from the beneficiaries.

To complement the efforts of CAG in tracking public funds, an effective advocacy strategy could be put in place to hold the government accountable to its commitments. This could entail empowering smallholder farmers' organisations to influence policies. The empowerment could involve providing them with information and giving them the skills and knowledge required to articulate issues to demand their rights. In addition, there has to be a paradigm shift and a public-private partnership should be embraced to implement public expenditure programmes to make them sufficiently targeted to enable smallholder farmers to capture their full benefits.

References

Bank of Tanzania (2009). Economic Bulletin for the quarter ending March 2009. Vol. XLI, No. 1.

Hazell, P., Haggblade, S., Kirsten, I. & Mkandawire, R. (2003) African agriculture: Past performance, future imperatives. Paper presented at the InWEnt, IFPRI, NEPAD, CTA Conference, Pretoria, South Africa (1–3 December).

Kulaba, M. (2009). How much can citizens know about their budget in Tanzania: Findings of the Open Budget Transparency Survey 2008. Paper presented at the Policy Forum breakfast talk (27 March).

Matee, A.Z. & Shem, M. (2005). A review of current policies and laws that touch on pastoralism in Tanzania (Commissioned by ERETO II).

Mukuti L.F. & Barasa T. (2008). CAADP Implementation steps at national and regional levels. A paper presented at All ACP Agricultural Programme Eastern and Southern Africa Consultative Kick-off Workshop, Dar es Salaam, Tanzania (17–20 June).

Regional Strategic Analysis and Knowledge Support System (ReSAKSS) (2009). *Is Africa on track to meet the CAADP 6 per cent growth target for agriculture?* http://www.resakss.org

Rønsholt, F., Mushi, R., Shallanda, B. & Assey, P. (2003). *Results-orientated expenditure management country study – Tanzania.* Working Paper No. 204. London: Overseas Development Institute (ODI).

Tanzania Fertiliser Company Ltd (TFC) (2006). *The Fertiliser Market and TFC'S Roles in the Sector: Development of the Fertiliser Market in Tanzania (1968–2005).*

The case for restrategising spending priorities to support small-scale farmers in South Africa

Ruth Hall and Michael Aliber

> The model we're following is totally inappropriate in the sense that ... because the amount we fund is so small, it becomes a case of political Smarties rather than effective use of resources. Who gets the money in the end is either a lotto or a case of political connections.
>
> (Provincial agriculture manager, Eastern Cape, 2009: pers. comm.)

Introduction

'Small-scale farmers' in South Africa have been subject to years of official neglect, despite numerous policies and programmes that proclaim the opposite. In particular, the dismantling of the Bantustan agricultural development corporations (for all their faults) in the 1990s left a vacuum in production and marketing support for the now-estimated 200,000 commercially oriented smallholder farmers and 2.5 million households practising agriculture for mainly subsistence purposes (Aliber & Hall, 2010), at precisely the time when the elaborate architecture of regulation and subsidies for white commercial farmers was rapidly dismantled. The past decade, and particularly the past five years or so, has seen the growth of budgets to provide direct support to black and disadvantaged farmers in the form of grants for infrastructure, production inputs and other items, and recently through an extension service 'recovery programme'. Yet evidence shows that most black farming households receive little if any support, largely as a result of the available resources being skewed towards certain farmers over others.

The needs and interests of small farmers have, however, climbed the political agenda in recent years, attracting new policy emphasis. Shifts in the ruling tripartite alliance have contributed to more left-leaning and pro-poor policy pronouncements in a number of spheres, particularly in a newfound priority placed on rural development, which became a ministerial portfolio for the first time in the Zuma administration in 2009. 'Rural development, food security and land reform' was one of the five priority areas listed in the ANC's election manifesto of 2009, which also committed the party to address food security and to 'Expand access to food production schemes in rural and peri-urban areas to grow their own food with implements, tractors, fertilizers and pesticides' (ANC, 2009). Under the heading of rural development, the manifesto declared that:

The ANC government will: Intensify the land reform programme to ensure that more land is in the hands of the rural poor and will provide them with technical skills and financial resources to productively use the land to create sustainable livelihoods and decent work in rural areas ... [and] expand [the] agrarian reform programme, which will focus on the systematic promotion of agricultural co-oper-atives throughout the value chain, including agro-processing in the agricultural areas. Government will develop support measures to ensure more access to mar-kets and finance by small farmers, including fencing and irrigation systems.(ANC, 2009)

At Polokwane, the ANC adopted wide-ranging resolutions on 'rural development, land reform and agrarian change' which set a new tone for the party's focus on rural poverty and on agriculture. The resolution included a commitment to 'imple-ment the Freedom Charter's call to help those working the land with implements, seed, tractors, infrastructure for irrigation and other forms of material support' and 'implement large-scale programmes to establish new smallholders and improve the productivity of existing small-scale and subsistence farmers, and to integrate small-holders into formal value chains and link them with markets' (ANC, 2007). It noted that:

Our programmes of rural development, land reform and agrarian change must be integrated into a clear strategy that seeks to empower the poor, particularly those who already derive all or part of their livelihoods from the exploitation of productive land. In line with the Freedom Charter's call that 'the land shall be shared among those who work it', the critical beneficiaries of change must be rural women, farm-dwellers, household producers in former Bantustans, small busi-nesses and rural entrepreneurs and residents of urban and peri-urban areas that wish to engage in agricultural livelihoods. (ANC, 2007)

Along with improved services and infrastructure, and strengthened implementation of laws in support of farm dwellers, two of the four pillars of the new programme would be:

(b) Fundamental changes in the patterns of land ownership through the redis-tribution of 30 per cent of agricultural land before 2014. This must include comprehensive support programmes with proper monitoring mechanisms to ensure sustainable improvements in livelihoods for the rural poor, farm workers, farm-dwellers and small farmers, especially women.

(c) Agrarian change with a view to supporting subsistence food production, expanding the role and productivity of modern small-holder farming and main-taining a vibrant and competitive agricultural sector.(ANC, 2007)

However, dramatic increases in budget allocations to agriculture over the past five years have made little dent in the chronic problem of under-investment in small-scale (i.e. black) agriculture in South Africa. This is because of the huge numbers of people who are engaged in agriculture, mostly on a small-scale, often part-time basis, and largely with little or no interaction with the official programmes ostensibly there to help them. The still largely-white commercial sector also gets little support.

Rather, the dearth of support for small-scale farmers is the product of the funnelling of available resources to 'emerging' and 'commercialising' small- and medium-scale black farmers. This strategy of 'picking winners' coincides to a large degree with the focus on beneficiaries of one particular land reform programme that was initially designed for precisely the purpose of creating a black commercial farming class: the Land Redistribution for Agricultural Development (LRAD) programme.

This chapter reviews overall trends in budget allocations in support of small-scale farmers in South Africa. It analyses a key government programme, namely, the Comprehensive Agricultural Support Programme (CASP), and provides an initial assessment of spending priorities within this programme, using some national data, together with data from interviews with implementers in the two provinces that have the largest number of small farmers, namely the Eastern Cape and Limpopo.

Trends in public budgeting and expenditure

Despite the occasional wobble, the amount of money spent by government on the agricultural sector has grown impressively since the mid-1990s. Figure 4.1 illustrates this is two ways. First, using data from the statistical annex to National Treasury's annual *Budget Review*, it shows the consolidated national and provincial expenditure on 'agriculture, forestry and fisheries', where land reform expenditure/budgets are included (this is the higher line with diamond markers). To the left of the vertical line, the data points represent expenditure (though for 2008/09 this was still an estimate), while to the right they represent the medium-term budget estimates. The data have been adjusted for inflation (and in future years for anticipated inflation) using the consumer price index; thus the upward trend is real: between 1996/97 and 2008/09, expenditure nearly trebled. Notwithstanding the dip between 2008/09 and 2009/10 (which is all the more surprising in light of the greater emphasis placed on rural development by the ANC government since the last elections) and bearing in mind that the projected increase from 2009/10 to 2010/11 may not take place, the increase is still significant. Having said that, the share of the total government budget going to agriculture in 2008/09 was only 2.3 per cent, far short of the African Union's Maputo Protocol benchmark of 10 per cent – although this benchmark may be less applicable to South Africa (where agriculture represents less than 3 per cent of GDP) than to other African countries such as Mozambique (where it accounts for 26 per cent) or Malawi (39 per cent).

The second series (the lower line with square markers) shows provincial agricultural expenditure only. The difference between the two series is partly due to the fact that the consolidated series includes expenditure by the national Department of Agriculture, however it also includes the Agricultural Research Council and other national-level parastatals, as well as expenditure on fisheries and forestry. Although this provincial series is quite a bit lower, its growth has still been substantial: between 1996/97 and 2008/09, expenditure rose by almost exactly a factor of 3.

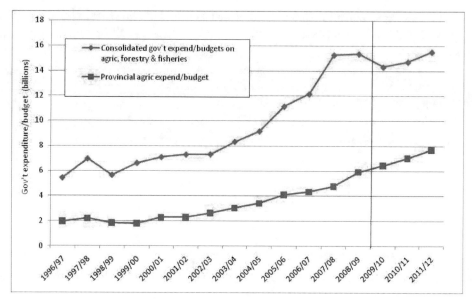

Figure 4.1: Agricultural sector expenditure/budgets (2008 Rand)
Sources: National Treasury (various) and National Treasury 2009b

However, although these are certainly significant increases, are these expenditure levels 'a lot'? One way of trying to gain perspective on the magnitude of these expenditure levels is to simply divide them by the number of agriculturalists. Given that there is little direct support to white commercial agriculture, we focus on the number of black farming households, which we estimate from Statistics SA's *Labour Force Survey*. In Figure 4.2 the higher line traces the per-household expenditure/budget based on the full consolidated budget for agriculture, forestry and fisheries, while the lower series does the same for the provincial agriculture spending. Using the first measure, the per-household expenditure in 2008/09 was about R5,700; by the second measure, it was R2,200. For the first measure, the increase between 2001/02 and 2008/09 was 71 per cent, while for the second, it was 46 per cent.

Given that, as of 2008, there were almost 2.7 million black farming households, this is no small achievement. Moreover, given that the vast majority of black farming households practise subsistence farming, a per-household expenditure of a few thousand rands seems reasonable; it is more than most such households spend on inputs in a typical year, but not extravagantly more.

However, what do we know about the actual distribution of this expenditure among farmers? We attempt to address this question in two ways: first in terms of the provincial disaggregation of expenditure, and second in terms of estimates as to numbers of farmers deriving *direct* benefits.

In terms of the provincial distribution of agricultural expenditure, the results are perhaps surprisingly equitable. Figure 4.3 presents the average annual expenditure per black farming household, by province, for the two periods 2001/02 through

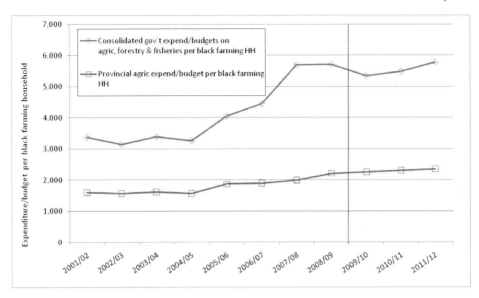

Figure 4.2: Agricultural sector expenditure/budgets per black farming household (2008 Rand)

Sources: National Treasury (various), National Treasury 2009b and Statistics SA (various)

2004/05, and 2005/06 through 2008/09. What the figure shows is that the average annual expenditure is remarkably even across provinces, with the obvious exceptions of Northern Cape and Western Cape, and the somewhat less obvious exception of North West. As for changes between the two periods, all provinces except Gauteng experienced an improvement, though oddly it was Northern Cape and Western Cape again that experienced the most significant improvements. The apparent inequity should not be exaggerated; Northern and Western Cape have relatively small numbers of black farming households, and together account for only 10 per cent of the total provincial expenditure for the second period. What this reveals above all is a job well done, in the sense that the distribution of expenditure for the most part mirrors the distribution of black farming households, which are overwhelmingly concentrated in the Eastern Cape (26 per cent), Limpopo (24 per cent) and KwaZulu-Natal (21 per cent).

However, a different picture emerges if we look in a little more depth as to what kinds of activities these budgets finance, and who is enjoying their benefits. Agricultural spending takes many forms, including extension services, infrastructure development through the Comprehensive Agricultural Support Programme (CASP), loans through the Micro Agricultural Financial Institutional Scheme of South Africa (MAFISA), and even research. Taking together extension, CASP and MAFISA, there is some reason for concern. First of all, averaging over the period 2005/06 through 2008/09, these three interventions collectively absorbed about 58 per cent of the total provincial expenditure.[1] However, from official delivery

---

[1] This is using 'compensation of employees' as an approximation for the cost of extension services.

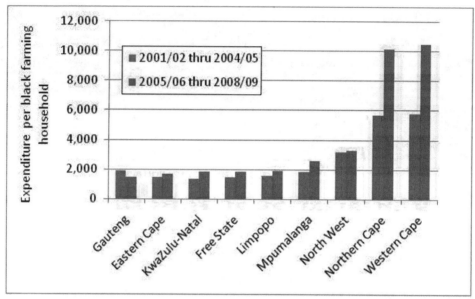

Figure 4.3: Agricultural sector expenditure/budgets per black farming household, by province (2008 Rand)

Sources: National Treasury 2009b and Statistics SA (various)

statistics, we know that during that four-year period, there was an annual average of about 61,000 beneficiaries of CASP (most of whom were land reform beneficiaries, as we will discuss in more detail later in the chapter), and about 2,500 loan recipients via MAFISA. As for the numbers of those benefiting from extension services, we have no recent data. The best indicator on offer is from Statistics SA's 1997 Rural Survey, which found that among those engaged in farming in the former homelands, only 11 per cent had had contact with an extension officer within the previous 12 months (Statistics SA, 1998). Given that the current total number of extension officers in the country is not very different from what it was then, we speculate that the share of black farming households receiving attention from extension staff is not very different today. (In addition, we have vast amounts of anecdotal evidence from around the country to back this up.)

What this means is that, in a given year, at most 13 per cent of black farming households are deriving direct benefits from the 58 per cent of the provincial spending made up from these three interventions.[2] While we must allow for the possibility that many farmers may derive indirect or passive benefits, and also acknowledge

---

As for the other 42 per cent of provincial expenditure, more than two thirds is 'goods and services', which is a form of current expenditure. What precisely this consists of is unclear, though presumably it covers transport costs of extension staff, office space, and so on. National Treasury's Provincial Budgets and Expenditure Review: 2005/06–2011/12 merely says of 'goods and services' that they '… are key to increasing agricultural productivity' (National Treasury, 2009b: 18).

[2] This is making the assumption that, for example, beneficiaries of CASP are not also beneficiaries of extension support, which in general is not the case.

that for CASP-funded infrastructure development in particular, the benefits should be enduring and thus not be measured strictly on a per annum basis, it still gives cause for concern. Take, for example, the R5.9 billion of provincial expenditure in 2008/09: this could be taken to mean that about 350,000 black farming households benefited from expenditure in the order of R17,000 each, while most of the other 2.3 million black households received benefits close to zero.

The biggest worry arguably is extension, in the sense that it already accounts for such a large share of provincial expenditure (not less than 50 per cent). How much larger would the extension service have to be to make an appreciable difference, i.e. to reach a significant number of black farmers?[3] And what would be the budget implications of a significantly larger and better extension service? Herein lies one of the key themes of this chapter: to the extent that fairly significant amounts of money are already being spent in the agricultural sector, and to the extent it is manifestly inadequate, where is there meaningful room for improvement?

The Comprehensive Agricultural Support Programme (CASP)

CASP was launched in 2004 with funds for disbursement to farming households. While clearly not the only, or largest, form of agricultural support, it is the most significant capital budget line potentially available to small-scale black farmers. CASP originated from the 2003 intergovernmental fiscal review of agriculture – conducted by National Treasury together with the Minister and MECs[4] – which found that agriculture was under-funded, and in particular experienced a gap in capital funding, as 80 per cent of total funding went on salaries. When CASP was created, there was a decision to keep it within the national department, rather than make it part of the equitable share to provinces, so as to ring-fence the funding from other priorities (NDA, 2007b). So although provincial departments implement the funding, they account directly to the national department on their expenditure on a quarterly basis, and submit province-level funding proposals for approval by the national department and minister.

The stated aim of CASP is: 'To expand the provision of support services, to pro-mote and facilitate agricultural development targeting beneficiaries of the Land Reform and other Agrarian Reform programmes' (NDA, 2007a). Initially conceived as a conditional grant targeting beneficiaries of land reform, CASP guidelines require that 70 per cent of funds go to land reform beneficiaries and the remain-ing 30 per cent to 'other agrarian reform beneficiaries' – in other words, those who already have some access to land, most likely people already living and farming at some scale in the communal areas of the former Bantustans (NDA, 2007a). In other words, although CASP is intended to address a wide variety of needs, in the views of many – especially officials and senior managers in the department of agriculture

---

[3]   Obviously, this is to say nothing about the quality of the current extension crops, which has been the focus of much concern in government in recent years (NDA, 2008b).

[4]   Members of the Executive Council – i.e. provincial ministers, in this case, of agriculture.

– it is essentially the 'agriculture' side of land reform. As Sam Malatji, then the department's national chief director of Land Development Services, observed at the national meeting to review the programme in 2007, 'CASP is the "AD" [agricultural development] in LRAD' (Malatji, 2007: pers. comm.).

The six 'pillars' of CASP for which funds may be made available are on- and off-farm infrastructure; information and knowledge management; training and capacity building; technical and advisory services; financing mechanisms; and marketing and business development. The only guide as to the weighting of these is that 10 per cent of CASP funds should go for household food production, 5 per cent for animal health, and 10 per cent for education, mentorship and training (NDA, 2007a).

CASP started with a total budget of R750 million for the first three years, escalating from R200 million in the first year of 2004/05, to R250 million the following year, and then rising to R300 million in 2006/07, after which it continued to rise more dramatically.

Table 4.1: CASP budget allocations, projects and beneficiaries, 2004/05 to 2009/10

Year	Budget (R million)	Percentage spent	Projects	Beneficiaries
2004/05	200	62%	510	46,500
2005/06	250	63%	1070	53,200
2006/07	300	84%	870	67,400
2007/08	415	85%	786	60,300
2008/09	535	90%	703	31,039
2009/10*	715			35,000
2010/11*	862			32,000
2011/12*	979			32,000

* Figures for 2009/10–2010/11 are projections.
Sources: DAFF 2009 and National Treasury 2009a

Allocations from the national department to each provincial department vary widely, and are supposed to be based on the number of land and agrarian reform beneficiaries/projects, the 'ruralness of the province', the size of agricultural land and arable land, and population size (NDA, 2007a). In practice, CASP forms part of a wider effort to provide Farmer Support, of which the most significant element (as noted above) is extension services (National Treasury, 2009b). In many provinces, in fact, CASP constitutes a fairly small proportion of the overall available budget. Table 4.2 shows the relatively low significance of CASP compared to overall provincial spending on Farmer Support in provinces such as Limpopo, KwaZulu-Natal and the Eastern Cape in 2008/09.

In the first two years of CASP, about 63 per cent of the allocation was spent (see Table 4.1). A degree of under-spending continued in the first few years and, despite not being able to disburse all the funds, provinces pushed for higher allocations,

Table 4.2: CASP budgets by province and as a percentage of Farmer Support budgets, 2008/09

Province	Farmer Support (in R millions)	CASP* (in R millions)	CASP as % of Farmer Support
Eastern Cape	511	90	18%
Free State	99	49	50%
Gauteng	71	25	36%
KwaZulu-Natal	646	88	14%
Limpopo	613	81	13%
Mpumalanga	350	53	15%
Northern Cape	72	37	51%
North West	150	68	46%
Western Cape	109	43	40%
TOTAL	2,622	535	20%

*CASP figures are allocations, not actual expenditures; for 2008/09, under-expenditure relative to allocations was 12 per cent nationally, with a low of 0 per cent for Mpumalanga and the Western Cape, and a high of 27 per cent for KwaZulu-Natal.
Sources: National Treasury 2009b and DAFF 2009

arguing that land reform was moving ahead and that many beneficiaries were not getting CASP support.

> Provinces claim that existing farmer support budgets are too small to meet all of these needs. In the context of under-spending (although the situation is improving) this position seems hard to justify. Although the demand/need for support in provinces is not contested, given that CASP in many instances only represents a small proportion of total farmers support budgets, the question of what the remaining farmer support budgets in the provinces are being used for needs to be answered first. Where it can be demonstrated that farmer support budgets are indeed inadequate, and where capacity to effectively implement exists, addition to farmer support budgets should be considered. (NDA, 2007b: 1)

The first review of CASP, conducted nationally in 2007, concluded that contrary to its name, CASP was not comprehensive either in its reach or in the types of support provided. In both respects, it was far from comprehensive: there were substantial barriers to access, prioritisation was unclear and inconsistent across provinces, usually with no clear rationale for prioritising one type of applicant over another, and even though there were six 'pillars' or focus areas for the kinds of support to be provided under the programme, in practice support forthcoming was almost entirely restricted to on-farm infrastructure. The other components of CASP (other than infrastructure) were not adequately explained to farmers. The review found that all provinces prioritised on-farm infrastructure over the other pillars of CASP, a pattern which the review deemed appropriate in some cases (such as the Northern Cape – presumably because of the importance of fencing and water points for grazing) and inappropriate in others (such as the Free State and Gauteng) (NDA, 2007b). With respect to the Eastern Cape, the review noted that CASP had only focused on on-farm infrastructure and that 'the other pillars of CASP do not really feature in the province' (NDA, 2007b:10).

> In all of the projects visited CASP has delivered infrastructure ranging from fencing, boreholes, watering points, irrigation infrastructure, livestock handling facilities, and structures such as packing sheds. Although appreciative of the infra-structure delivered (bar some concerns regarding quality), the needs of farmers are more comprehensive. As in other provinces though there is a call for a wider basket of services to be made available through CASP. (NDA, 2007b:10)

The CASP review found that implementation was characterised by fragmented planning, a backlog of SLAG and LRAD projects awaiting CASP funds, separate approval mechanisms for land acquisition and agricultural support, complicated procurement procedures and inadequate capacity and access to information (presumably among both potential beneficiaries and the officials administering the programme) (NDA, 2007a). It concluded that, underlying these were two major problems. The first was one of programme administration, specifically the 'lengthy and bureaucratic planning and budgeting process which mitigates against prompt and timeous service delivery', compounded by cumbersome procurement processes (NDA, 2007b:1). The second was programme access, which as the review noted, was a 'mixed picture':

> Many of the current beneficiaries were not centrally involved in the application process – much of this was done for beneficiaries by agriculture (or in some cases land affairs) staff. For those outside of the programme the issues was [sic] more problematic. Although many had heard of CASP, many were unaware of how one gained access to it. There was confusion among farmers as to what CASP is. Many, who are not land reform beneficiaries, require broader and general agricultural support services. (NDA 2007b:1)

The CASP review noted the variable practices across provinces in terms of who is prioritised – and appeared to favour the allocation of most CASP funds to land reform projects rather than other farmers, implying that other farmer support funds should go to non-land reform beneficiaries, and noting a danger that land reform would be crowded out by the sheer scale of the needs of existing farmers in communal areas.

At present, in some provinces the predominant focus is on land reform, but in others this interpretation is challenged, and without controls there is a tendency for CASP monies to slip toward those. It is critical that a common understanding of who CASP is targeted at and why is ingrained in the programme. There is a real danger that CASP will simply become a hold-all programme addressing needs that should actually be dealt with through broader provincial farmer support budgets. (NDA 2007b:2)

The review found that there were major problems with bureaucratically determined processes of planning, approval and procurement, in that these are at odds with the cyclical nature of agriculture. It also found that the focus of CASP was heavily contested in some provinces – for instance, what weight should be given to land reform beneficiaries versus other black farmers (both poor semi-subsistence farmers in the communal areas, and 'emerging' or commercialising black farmers).

The absence of strategy: Practices of disbursement in CASP

National project data for CASP allocations in 2009/10 (kindly provided by the National Department of Agriculture for the purpose of this analysis) show great variation both between and within provinces. Funding per project ranges from R20,000 (for irrigation infrastructure) to R5.4 million (for a poultry house), and, in addition, a high proportion of projects benefit more than once – for example, receiving funds in two or three consecutive years.

Allocation of CASP funds is highly skewed to a small proportion of beneficiaries. Analysis of the national data shows that, among the 322 projects funded in 2009, for which beneficiary data are available, *79.8 per cent of CASP expenditure went to 20 per cent of the beneficiaries, or, worse, 50.7 per cent went to 2.6 per cent of the*

Table 4.3: CASP allocations for 2009/10 by province

	Number of projects	Total allocation (in R'000)	Percentage of total allocation
Eastern Cape	110	149,268	22
Free State	127	65,659	10
Gauteng	154	24,734	4
KwaZulu-Natal	197	94,487	14
Limpopo	156	108,453	16
Mpumalanga	22	55,504	8
Northern Cape	17	36,451	5
North West	51	91,518	13
Western Cape	121	63,640	9
TOTAL	955	689,714	100

Source: NDA 2009

beneficiaries. Given that those receiving CASP support in 2009 accounted for less than 1 per cent of small-scale farmers, this suggests that the lion's share of state funding for small-scale farmers went to fewer than 0.02 per cent of them.

Further, the variation is astonishing between the provinces, with Mpumalanga, the Northern Cape and the North West having far fewer projects than the other provinces – even when taking into account that the allocations to these provinces are low compared to the other provinces (with the exception of Gauteng). While a smaller number of projects do not necessarily indicate that fewer people are being assisted, in some instances this seems to be the case.

Mpumalanga, Northern Cape and North West have on the whole fewer larger (i.e. more expensive) projects – though major projects are found in all provinces, even those like the Eastern Cape and Limpopo where a larger number of medium-sized projects are to be found. But there are also cases of very substantial transfers of funds to few people, in those provinces which report on numbers of beneficiaries per project (Eastern Cape, Limpopo and North West do not do so). For example, a broiler house project in Mpumalanga, benefiting 12 people, cost R10.8 million – the largest single project expenditure in the country in 2009. In the same province, a woman and a man (perhaps related to one another) were together allocated R497,000, also for a broiler house project, while in the Free State one woman got R270,000 to renovate her poultry houses. A large portion of projects in Gauteng were for one individual farmer, averaging about R200,000 each. These examples illustrate the permissiveness rather than directive nature of policy in this area – there is no requirement to demonstrate need, nor is there any prescribed rationale according to which those assessing the applications (usually district screening committees) should decide on how to distribute funds across competing and non-equivalent needs. It is unsurprising, therefore, that such widely divergent practices have emerged.

Within provinces there is, of course, a variety of projects, some of which involve major infrastructure, but most of which are 'on-farm' infrastructure rather than, for instance, shared infrastructure designed to serve the needs of a community of producers in a given area engaged in similar types of production. There are exceptions, such as the dipping tanks in communal areas in Limpopo and major irrigation infrastructure in the Eastern Cape, but by and large, infrastructure is limited to private on-farm infrastructure and, as a result, to privately-owned land – and therefore to land reform projects rather than communal areas – a theme to which we now turn.

Competing and unequal priorities: Land reform and communal areas

In practice, a major reason why communal areas are largely excluded from CASP funding is the combination of three factors: the equation of CASP with 'infrastructure', the lack of secure tenure in communal areas on which to build this infrastructure, and the political priority attached to improving the perceived performance of land reform projects. In the absence of certainty about the land rights of beneficiaries – to own and control the infrastructure created with the CASP funds allocated to them – agricultural officials are somewhat at a loss as to how to support farmers in these areas. Instead, 'food security' funds are channelled to provide 'starter packs' of seed and implements.

The CASP manager for Limpopo explained that, without farmers having secure tenure rights on communal land, CASP cannot be provided for fixed infrastructure – though arguably the department is not under any formal obligation to require such evidence in order to disburse funds.

> We move from a principle that says, in each district at least 75 per cent of the CASP budget must go to land reform projects. We'll still provide for the communal land, as long as the land tenure issues are clear. The normal PTO [permission to occupy certificate] is not legislated as such, and the tenure is not well documented, the chief just says that you are given a piece of land to do agriculture. So we have moved to discuss with chiefs, and we have come up with some kind of leases that talk to the exact size and extent of that piece of land, so in that way we are starting to move towards [providing CASP support on] communal land. (Provincial CASP manager, 2009: pers. comm.)

Similarly, in the Eastern Cape implementers are concerned that the majority of small black farmers cannot access support through CASP because of the priority placed on land reform (i.e. projects outside the communal areas) and on fixed infrastructure, which requires that the beneficiary own the land in question (which also has the effect of excluding many farmers in the former Ciskei and Transkei regions). The bulk of funds go to a relatively small number of land reform beneficiaries on commercial farms, yet in the Eastern Cape, agricultural officials argue that the priority should be fencing and water systems in the former Transkei, as these are the most critical infrastructure needs.

> We have been fighting it, [the] 70% to land reform beneficiaries, but they are relaxing from that. Because we are saying our biggest need is in the former Transkei [i.e. communal] areas. But because we don't have any other funding, we use the CASP … OR Tambo [district] gets a very small part of CASP because very little of it is commercial farmland, so they fall within the 30% part – also Amathole, Alfred Nzo, Chris Hani – they have no land reform land. The proportion (of farmers getting CASP support) is much higher among land reform beneficiaries [than it is among farmers in the communal areas]. (Provincial agriculture manager, 2009: personal communication.)

Similarly, those getting leases on state-owned land through the Proactive Land Acquisition Strategy (PLAS) in the Eastern Cape have found that this is incompatible with the requirements of MAFISA, in that MAFISA requires that, for a standard five-year loan, the applicant must have security of tenure for five years – whereas under the PLAS scheme the farmer only gets a lease agreement for three years, so their applications are rejected. As a result, there are a number of people who have been allocated land through PLAS and are unable to buy livestock as they are not eligible for state support in the form of either MAFISA loans or CASP grants because they are considered to have inadequate tenure for collateral purposes (provincial agriculture manager, 2009: pers. comm.)

The option of providing 'off-farm' infrastructure in communal areas – i.e. infrastructure that can serve a community or group of producers engaged in similar production in a given area – is the obvious way around the obstacle of insecure tenure (if indeed it is an obstacle). However, it appears that there is no mechanism for agricultural officials to create such infrastructure in the absence of a 'business plan' submitted by an 'applicant'. This is frequently presented as a reason why this avenue has not been more actively explored, although in reality CASP applications are often initiated by officials, following land transfers under land reform, rather than by 'farmers'.

'Commercial viability': The presumed criterion

Though the criterion of 'commercial viability' appears nowhere in the CASP policy (which focuses instead on sustainability), implementers in these two provinces prioritise this factor consistently – in fact express it as an essential precondition for allocation of CASP funds.

> At this stage, there are still some debates, what in actual fact we should call the sustainability or the viability of projects. This is a debate of the department every year, but we take time to come up with a final approach. It has been there in this team that has been identified, it will deal with the issues of, if you say there is viability in the project, what do you mean? Like if there is a turnover of half a million, or if the project is servicing its debts – so we are deciding what will be our indicator … [and it should be] not high profit margin, but the ability of these guys monthly to service their debts. But we don't have that guideline as yet, but that [once we've clarified this] will help us and serve as our indicators for good performance or non-performance. (CASP manager, Limpopo 2009: pers. comm.)

As a result, CASP has become bifurcated between food security for farmers in communal areas and infrastructure for farmers in the commercial farming districts. In Limpopo, all 'food security' and 'animal health' allocations were for communal areas, while 92 per cent of 'infrastructure' allocations were for land reform projects outside these areas. LRAD is not considered to be 'food security'; as the Limpopo manager observed, '10 per cent of our budget is for food security, and that 10 per cent will normally go to the small-scale farmers in the communal land. Because you cannot say that the budget for food security should go to LRAD and the like' (CASP manager, Limpopo, 2009: pers. comm.). The presumption that land reform is a sphere of potential 'commercial viability' while communal areas are for 'food security' is put forward by agricultural officials as a rationale for prioritising the former. They acknowledge that their own criteria for assessing business plans set 'commercial viability' as a precondition for approving funds.

> It is not a very good formula that is written down, but each year, we look at how much land has been transferred [through land reform], and what the requirements are, and what the market is, which talks to our principles of development – which

is a commodity and value chain approach and the like. (CASP manager, Limpopo, 2009: pers. comm.)

Handing out 'political Smarties': Rationing scarce resources

The land redistribution process, since its inception (and at least up to the creation of the proactive land acquisition strategy), was structured around a central concern to ration resources according to a defined logic – initially providing grants at a level pegged to the housing subsidy (at R15,000, later rising to R16,000 and then extending across a sliding scale from R20,000 to R100,000 per applicant, depending on the level of 'own contribution').

Under CASP, however, there is no restriction or cap on the maximum amount of public support that a person or a project can receive. In Limpopo, an implementer acknowledged that, with no guidelines whatsoever governing the distribution of resources, 'we have recently seen a lot of abuse of that leniency', but went on to comment that 'at present we have no guidelines for funding; if there is a request that is for a business that is sound, it has markets, it is within the plans for CASP, then we will fund it' (CASP manager, Limpopo 2009: pers. comm.).

In the absence of any prescription about equity, agricultural officials are subject to institutional pressures to crowd in resources rather than distribute these widely. As an agricultural department manager in the Eastern Cape observed, there are good reasons why fewer projects – which may or may not involve fewer people – are preferable from a bureaucratic point of view.

> The model we're following is totally inappropriate in the sense that ... because the amount we fund is so small, it becomes a case of political Smarties rather than effective use of resources. Who gets the money in the end is either a lotto or a case of political connections. If our budget were to increase to R550 million a year and if we reduce the funding level to 60 per cent [of costs, by leveraging private resources], it would still take us 100 years [to make up the funding backlog for infrastructure]. What we're spending on infrastructure is less than a drop in the ocean... The impact on agriculture is negligible. (Provincial agriculture manager, Eastern Cape, 2009: pers. comm.)

Combined with the imperative to spend large budgets, and the complexity of doing so through many smaller projects rather than fewer bigger projects, implementers are under pressure to scale down the number of projects and scale up the size of each project.

> There's no cap on individuals – they can get anything from R20,000 up to R9 million – there are no guidelines. We got a lot of flak for that. We have had about 120 – 130 projects in the Eastern Cape, so the policy being pushed from national is to cut down projects, maybe to just six for the province, or one per municipality, in order to speed up administration. To administer R10 is as much as to administer R10 million, so we are meant to do fewer, bigger projects. The more projects you have, the more work you have. (Provincial agriculture manager, 2009: pers. comm.)

The Eastern Cape tried to follow a strategy adopted in the Western Cape, of outsourcing CASP distribution to a private sector implementing agent, in order to circumvent the need for tender committees and short-circuit procurement processes – but has had to abandon this after a critical response from the provincial auditors. 'We are trying to do something for which government is not designed. Procurement systems are not for service delivery; they're there to account for public funds. For every rand [of CASP money], it costs at least three times more to spend it properly (provincial agriculture manager, Eastern Cape, 2009: pers. comm.). The tendency in some provinces to disburse large amounts to few projects (and people) may have to do with these pressures, but it also, crucially, leaves the system open to abuse in the form of political patronage and corruption.

In the absence of any rationing mechanism – or any limit on allocations – CASP also fails to leverage resources in major commercial projects (where beneficiaries may be able to contribute some of their own capital and to access loans), while neglecting modest needs among the majority of small farmers. Given the limited funds available for small farmers, a major criticism then is not only one of equity, but one of leveraging resources. Under CASP, government is offering up to 100 per cent grants to commercial ventures – rather than providing partial subsidies and leveraging commercial farmers' own resources – while often providing nothing to subsistence producers. 'The way we are doing CASP, we need our heads read as a country. First, we are funding things 100 per cent, which in most cases is completely inappropriate … That's a paradigm we've got to change, for one' (provincial agriculture manager, Eastern Cape, 2009: pers. comm.).

Conclusion

Despite the strong political and policy support for small-scale farmers in South Africa, and despite significant increases in agricultural budgets over the past decade or so, the support currently rendered to small-scale farmers is not consistent with the visions espoused in political and policy statements. This chapter has sought to present the reasons why – in part by examining national expenditure trends, and in part by focusing on one particular intervention, namely, the Comprehensive Agricultural Support Programme (CASP).

We conclude that dramatic increases in public expenditure support to small-scale agriculture are highly unlikely, while further incremental increases to support the sector will, in themselves, make little difference. The inadequacy of the current support measures to small-scale farmers is most vividly illustrated by the fact that only a very small portion of small-scale, black farmers in South Africa in fact benefit from such support in a typical year – about 13 per cent according to our estimate. Is this a case of simply too little money being allocated to the sector? To some extent, yes: even though there have been significant increases, these are relative to the low base established by the massive withdrawal of public funding for agriculture in the mid-1980s.

CASP expenditure has grown in leaps and bounds, and now represents the bulk of funding that is explicitly available for capital expenditure to support small-scale farmers. However, this chapter demonstrates how the overall 'footprint' of CASP has shrunk in proportion to the rise in its budget, and even in nominal terms – fewer people are benefiting than when CASP started. The reason has to do with political pressure to produce commercial success stories in land reform, combined with the bureaucratic impetus to spend ever-larger proportions of CASP support on ever-smaller numbers of farmers. This process exactly mirrors the trends in respect of land redistribution, to which CASP is closely related. While it might appear perverse, the pattern is also understandable: subjected to harsh criticism for under-expenditure, implementers have found the path of least resistance.

Our analysis shows that the primary constraint in state support to small-scale farmers is not the level of budget, but the misallocation of funds. Instead of 2.7 million 'average black farming households' receiving R2,200 worth of benefits per year, our data suggests instead that each year anything between 50 and 200 households are receiving over R500,000 each (largely in the form of CASP support), about 350,000 are receiving R17,000 (in the form of extension advice and other services), while 2.3 million households are receiving close to R0. As a result, much of the money already available to support small-scale agriculture is not well spent, with a particular imbalance evident between relatively large amounts of support to rather few 'new farmers' in badly conceptualised land reform projects, at the expense of the many existing black farmers within the ex-Bantustans.

The reality is that supporting small-scale farmers is difficult and labour-intensive. While there is definitely a need for increased capital expenditure, doing this well requires attention to equity in distributing scarce funds, as well as time, cogent planning, and perhaps more patience. On the other hand, the fact that CASP is dependent on extension services, while extension services reach too small a share of small-scale farmers, means that CASP is almost structurally unable to reach large numbers of small-scale farmers. And yet, despite absorbing a very large share of provincial agricultural expenditure, extension reaches limited numbers of agriculturalists – and the quality of extension advice is also uneven and reportedly poor in some cases. Doubling the extension corps would still result in an inadequate extension corps, reaching only a minority of agriculturalists, and it would cost more than the State is probably prepared to commit.

The conclusion, therefore, is that we are currently at an impasse. Increasing CASP budgets will accomplish little, because the vision of CASP is excessively oriented to supporting individual farmers, is excessively channelled into land reform projects (the design of which is in need of a dramatic overhaul, in the absence of which CASP support to them will continue to be a case of 'throwing good money after bad'), and is dependent on an extension service that is itself equipped to serve only a minority of small-scale farmers and cannot be feasibly scaled up.

The only way out of the impasse would appear to be to use the resources currently at our disposal in more effective ways. In respect of CASP, there is an urgent need to shift the emphasis of support from on-farm infrastructure and inputs to community-level infrastructure, market development and institutional re-engineering. The current model of funding, which focuses on one-on-one assistance at 'project' level, is limited in its impact, cannot feasibly be scaled up and does not lend itself to indivisible public goods and regulation, which are effective ways of benefiting large numbers of producers, and which are among the key forms of support that in the past were used to develop the white farming sector. As for refashioning extension services, this is the larger challenge: it will require, above all, experimenting with models that have the potential to greatly stretch the reach of our limited number of extension officers.

References

Aliber, M. & Hall R. (2010). *Development of Evidence-based Policy around Small-scale Farming.* Report commissioned by the Programme to Support Pro-Poor Policy Development, on behalf of the Presidency.

ANC (African National Congress) (2007). *Resolution on Rural Development, Land Reform and Agrarian Change.* 52nd National Conference, Polokwane, Limpopo, December 2007.

ANC (African National Congress) (2009). *ANC Election Manifesto: Working together we can do more.* www.anc.org.za, accessed April 2009.

DAFF (Department of Agriculture, Forestry and Fisheries) (2009). Comments on the FFC recommendations on the division of revenue 2010/11. Presentation to the Select Committee on Finance. [PowerPoint presentation] 7 August 2009.

Latsatsi-Duba (2009). MEC Letsatsi-Duba delivers Budget Speech 2009/10. Limpopo Department of Agriculture, 23 June 2009.

National Treasury (various years). *Budget Review.* Pretoria: Government Printer.

National Treasury (2009a). Budget Vote 23: Agriculture. In: *Estimates of National Expenditure 2009/10.* Pretoria: Government Printer: pp. 509–32.

National Treasury (2009b). *Provincial Budgets and Expenditure Review: 2005/06–2011/12.* Pretoria: Government Printer.

Magazdi, D. (2008). Limpopo Department of Agriculture Budget Speech 2008/09. Delivered by MEC Dikeledi Magadzi. [Electronic document]. No date or place.

NDA (National Department of Agriculture) (2007a). Comprehensive Agricultural Support Programme (CASP): Background on CASP. Presented at the National Review Meeting, Pretoria. [PowerPoint presentation] 20 February 2007.

NDA (National Department of Agriculture) (2007b). A national review of the Comprehensive Agricultural Support Programme by Umhlaba Rural Services. Pretoria: NDA, March 2007.

NDA (National Department of Agriculture) (2008a). Comprehensive Agricultural Support Programme. [PowerPoint presentation]. Presentation to the Portfolio Committee on Agriculture and Land Affairs, 20 February 2008.

NDA (National Department of Agriculture) (2008b). The state of Extension and Advisory Service within the Agricultural Public Service: A need for recovery. Internal report.

NDA (National Department of Agriculture) (2009). 2009/10 Provincial CASP project list. Electronic data: [Excel spreadsheet]. Obtained from National CASP Office, NDA, Pretoria, 6 November 2009.

Nkwinti, G. (2008). Eastern Cape Department of Agriculture 2008 Policy Speech, delivered by Gugile Nkwinti, Bisho, Eastern Cape, 11 March 2008.

Sogoni, M. (2009). Eastern Cape Department of Agriculture and Rural Development Budget and Policy Speech for 2009/10, delivered by MEC M. Sogoni. Bhisho, Eastern Cape, 18 June 2009.

Stats SA (Statistics South Africa) (1998). *Rural Survey.* Electronic data set.

Stats SA (Statistics South Africa) (various years). *Labour Force Survey.* Electronic data sets.

Interviews

Agriculture manager, Eastern Cape Department of Agriculture. Telephonic interview, 2 November 2009.

Agriculture manager, Limpopo Department of Agriculture. Telephonic interview, 5 November 2009.

Sam Malatji, Chief Director of Land Development Services, National Department of Agriculture. CASP National Review Meeting, Protea Hotel, Pretoria, 20 February 2007.

Challenges of smallholder farmers' participation in agricultural policies in eastern and southern Africa: The experience of ESAFF

Joe Mzinga

Introduction

The eastern and southern African (ESA) region is home to about 300 million people. In all of these countries, from Kenya to Lesotho, from Malawi to Zimbabwe and from Tanzania to Burundi, 60 to 80 per cent of the population are smallholder farmers who live in rural areas. These farmers are crop growers, fisher-folk and livestock keepers. Although these people account for the majority of the population, they are not adequately involved in decision-making and the policy processes that touch their daily lives.

Whereas other groups and communities such as gender and women activists, business people, trade unions and NGOs have at least managed to find rightful space to engage with decision-making bodies at national and regional levels, poor smallholder farmers in rural areas are still not visible in decision-making processes. Most of the ongoing agricultural strategies and programmes are hardly based on the needs and aspirations of smallholder farmers, as their involvement in policy formulation has been too artificial and ad hoc. Those who participate as proxy are mainly local or international NGOs, researchers or local business community members working with smallholder farmers.

Most smallholder farmers are not aware of the national, regional and continental initiatives on agriculture. The Comprehensive Africa Agriculture Development Programme (CAADP) and the Maputo Declaration have remained the vocabulary of elites, government officials and few business people.

If agricultural policies and strategies are to work and produce intended results, stakeholders (smallholder farmers) have to be involved in the designing, implementation and monitoring of these strategies. This is what can be called real or genuine participation. The situation in many countries in the ESA region is better today than it was during the 1980s and 1990s. Today, democratisation, decentralisation, free speeches and the widespread use of communication technologies such as the Internet and mobile phone has transformed the region. There is now an opportunity for smallholder farmers and the poor to be heard in the political arena.

Defining participation, stakeholders

In development work, people use 'participation' to denote involvement, owner-ship and power sharing, creating synergies and thinking and working together for mutual benefit. The principles of participation include involvement, building on existing structures, appreciating gender and diversity and the uniqueness of each situation, using every opportunity to learn, observing and taking initiative, and communicating and sharing ideas.

In the context of this chapter, participation means taking part in the conceptuali-sation, formulation, implementation and monitoring of policy as a true partner and not as a stooge. Participation means bringing change from within. It means being informed of what is expected of one, and being asked to contribute one's views. Participation means being part of the implementation process either as an active entity (deliverer) or passive entity (observer or monitor). And finally participa-tion means having the right to evaluate the effectiveness, efficiency and impact of a policy. In many countries in the ESA region, the general political environment is favourable to engagement on agricultural policies and issues.

Who are the stakeholders?

In this context, stakeholders mean an individual or groups of people with com-mon and direct interest in a specific issue. The major stakeholders in agriculture in the ESA region are the smallholder farmers or small producers. Small producers are crop growers, livestock keepers and fisher-folk. Smallholder farmers or small producers live on subsistence crop farming, subsistence livestock keeping and sub-sistence fishing. For these are people, subsistence farming is a way of life.

Why participation matters

True participation matters in policy processes, because that is where the people's will can be heard and heeded. Participation in governance structures can ensure the required changes in policy practices. Participating out of the system cannot guaran-tee changes in policy unless it is backed by mass public opinion, mass movement or mass demonstration.

Participation in policy processes is important because many policies have a direct impact on smallholder farmers. It is vital that civil society participates in policy formulation, especially since the introduction of Poverty Reduction Strategy (PRS) in the 1990s, and the market economy and multi-party democracies. Civil society plays a number of roles in the national and local budgeting processes, despite the fact that its formal role (participation in the Public Expenditure Review (PER) processes) is limited to a consultative one. Informal roles include analysing public budgets, producing simplified and popular versions of the budget and related documents, playing a watchdog role, tracking expenditure at the local level, and advocating for improvements in terms of specific issues and overall transparency and accountability. Civil society's informal roles are more effective when they go hand in hand with the strategic use of the media and popular citizen engagement.

Participation of farmers' organisations at local government level

Ideally, effective participation of smallholder farmers in agricultural policies should focus on five levels. The first level is the local government level. The decentralisation processes, through the Local Government Reform Programmes (LGRP), that are taking place in many ESA countries, are affording individuals and groups the opportunity to make an impact. This means that smallholder farmers can influence policies and resource allocation (budgets) and other issues at district levels. These LGRPs are aimed at reducing the proportion of people living in abject poverty by enabling them to elect their local leaders, and to hold them to account for quality, access and equitable delivery of public services.

Participation of farmers' organisations at ministerial level

The second level at which participation matters is at national level. At this level there are many important actors, such as the ministries of agriculture, fisheries and livestock, to ensure that the voices of smallholder farmers are heard. Other important ministries are those responsible for land issues, finance and local government.

The Ministry of Agriculture is important because it is key to the implementation of agriculture development programmes. Many countries have agriculture development strategies which are financed using domestic tax payers' money or external finance from development partners (donor countries). This ministry (like those of fisheries and livestock) is also responsible for the submission of budget estimates to the ministries of planning and finance.

The Ministry of Finance plays a central role in resource allocation (budgeting) It makes projections, sets ceilings for budget allocations, negotiates priorities with all departments, collects revenues (with revenue authorities) and disburses funds. This ministry also plays an important controlling function through the Accountant General (in some countries like Tanzania), who is responsible for ensuring that all financial transactions and reporting is done according to the proper regulations (HakiElimu and Policy Forum, *Understanding the Budget Process in Tanzania*).

Engaging parliamentarians

Another important organ in agricultural policy processes is Parliament. Parliaments in ESA countries play a major role in running the affairs of the country. The functions of Parliament are enshrined in the constitution of each country. Parliament is the principal organ, with the authority, on behalf of the people, to oversee and advise the government and all its organs in the discharge of their respective responsibilities. The main function of Parliament is to enact laws that govern the country and to ensure that the government meets its obligations to the citizenry. Because it is impossible to engage every parliamentarian, it is important to engage with selected standing committees, particularly those related to public finance, agriculture and rural development.

Although Parliament does not have the power to amend the budget in Tanzania or to reallocate funds, it can refuse to adopt the budget presented by the executive, although the consequences of this step are profound: the President has the constitutional power to dissolve Parliament in response.

Members of Parliament (MPs) have an important role to play. They are tasked to represent their constituencies in the National Assembly and to discuss issues, problems and challenges that face the people. The aim is to ensure that these problems are known by the relevant authorities and that plans are put in place to solve these. An MP can present issues from his/her constituency during question sessions, and he/she also has the right to ask to be given a copy of answers from a particular ministry.

Smallholder farmers' organisations and civil society organisations (CSOs) can play a major role in conducting research on the issues and problems that face them and present this to relevant standing committees or an individual MP. In all five East African countries, the national budgets are read on the same day in June each year. This affords farmer organisations and other stakeholders the opportunity to see whether their inputs at local government (grassroots) level have been reflected in the national budget. In southern Africa many countries present their budgets between December and January each year.

Participation of farmers' organisations at the regional economic grouping level

With growing globalisation and regionalisation, continental groups and economic blocs have become an important for making decisions which are implemented at national level. Examples include the Economic Partnership Agreements (EPAs) between Africa and the European Union, the Comprehensive Africa Agriculture Development Programme (CAADP), and the Dar es Salaam Declaration on Food Security and Rural Development of 2004, in which governments committed themselves to allocate 10 per cent of their national budgets to agriculture by 2009 (which disappointingly didn't happen, but which was reaffirmed in Sirte, Libya, with a new deadline of 2015).

In ESA, there are several major economic groupings with which smallholder farmers can engage. These include the East African Community, based in Arusha, Tanzania; the Common Market for Eastern and Southern Africa (COMESA), with the secretariat in Lusaka, Zambia, and the Southern African Development Community (SADC), with headquarters in Gaborone, Botswana.

A number of regional economic development programmes exist, with strong agricultural development components. These include SADC's Regional Indicative Strategic Development Plan (RISDP), NEPAD's Comprehensive Africa Agriculture

Development Programme (CAADP) and COMESA's Agriculture Policy (CAP). Although various stakeholders have been involved in the development of regional agricultural development frameworks and policies, including trade protocols, the input from farmer organisations has been weak, disjointed and rather limited. The underlying causes for this include the lack of effective representation of farmers at the regional level, the limited capacity of Southern Africa Confederation of Agricultural Unions (SACAU) to address regional and international agricultural development issues and inadequate capacity of national farmer organisations (FOs) to develop and articulate their positions.

This means that even civil society, including farmer organisations, have to engage government at regional and continental levels to advance their causes.

Participation of farmers' organisations at the African Union level

There are good reasons for civil society and smallholder farmers' networks to engage with the African Union (AU). It is the highest inter-governmental organisation for the African continent, responsible for promoting Africa's social, political, economic and cultural development, among other things.

The African Union (AU) has committed to a vision of Africa that is 'integrated, prosperous and peaceful … driven by its own citizens, a dynamic force in the global arena'.

Smallholder farmers' engagement at African Union level is important for two reasons: it can enable them to get updated on upcoming issues in order to lobby at regional or country level; secondly, AU-level engagement helps to expand and enhance networking among like-minded organisations. At AU level some CSOs on the continent, especially those working in areas of peace (The Darfur Consortium), gender (women's rights coalitions), HIV/AIDS, human rights and development (Oxfam) have managed to penetrate and influence the AU. By 2009, about 49 African NGOs had been granted observer status within the AU. To get observer status, an NGO has to be registered in an African state, must have been operational for at least three years, and have a democratically adopted constitution. But the most challenging requirement is that the NGO must have two thirds funding from its own members. The Economic, Social and Cultural Council (ECOSOCC), which is an official advisory organ within the AU structure, is designed to be a platform for CSOs in Africa to engage the AU. The office of the African Citizen's and Diaspora Directorate (of the AU Commission) provides another window for CSOs in Africa to engage and influence the African Union.

In the past there has been a lack of concerted effort on the part of smallholder farmers and farmer organisations to engage with the AU. Slowly this is changing. The Pan African Farmers' Forum initiative in eastern Africa and the Pan African Platform for the Farmer of Africa initiative in West Africa are two examples of the efforts to bring farmers organisations together to speak with one voice. This process has tended to sideline the involvement of real smallholder farmers and seems to be a top-down approach.

Issues of concern at African Union level

It is important for smallholder farmers organisations to engage the African Union (AU) to speed up the implementation of policies and declarations made at the AU level. For instance, the Maputo Declaration called for countries to increase their budget allocation to agriculture and food security to 10 per cent, but this has not happened in most African countries.

The Sirte Declaration adopted by the Thirteenth Ordinary Session of the Assembly in Sirte, Libya, in July 2009, committed countries to scale up their investment in agriculture for economic growth and food security, in an effort to accelerate the implementation of the CAADP agenda at the country level. African heads of state and the African Union recommitted their countries to the Maputo Declaration, to allocate at least 10 per cent of their annual national budgets to the agricultural sector by 2015. This reaffirmed the important role of agriculture in national development strategies. The declaration emphasised that smallholder-friendly value-chain development and access to markets and financial services should be key elements to enhancing financial sustainability and growth of the agricultural sector and related wealth creation.

In Sirte, African leaders promised to meet their individual and collective responsibility and commitment to provide necessary leadership on comprehensive and Africa-wide approaches to address the root causes of poverty and hunger, and to accelerate progress to achieve the growth and budgetary targets set out in the CAADP. They said they were keen to support relevant policy and institutional reforms that would stimulate and facilitate accelerated expansion of agriculture-related market opportunities by modernising domestic and regional trading systems, removing obstacles to trans-border trades, and increasing smallholder farmers' access to inputs and the necessary commercial infrastructure and technical skills to fully integrate them into the growing value chains.

Despite the Maputo Declaration of 2003, most of the African states had failed to meet the commitment to allocate 10 per cent of their national budgets to agriculture by the year 2008.

Some countries that are above the CAADP 10 per cent target are shown in Table 5.1 (see following page). EAS countries that are above the 5 per cent target are: Malawi, Rwanda, Mozambique, Madagascar, Zambia, Zimbabwe, Tanzania and Namibia.

Those that are below the 5 per cent target are: Uganda, Swaziland, Kenya, Burundi, Botswana, Rwanda, Lesotho, Mauritius and Democratic Republic of Congo (DRC).

Given this failure, African farmers should speak with one voice at AU level, as well as at regional economic bloc and country level to put pressure on head of states and governments to meet their commitments. It is equally important to monitor the utilisation of funds allocated to agriculture, but farmer organisations have experienced a lack of capacity and a lack of funding to enable them carry out the required advocacy and monitoring.

Table 5.1: Some countries above the CAADP 10 per cent of their national budgets.

Country	Percentage
Burkina Faso	20%
Niger	15%
Guinea	13.5%
Malawi	12%
Ethiopia	11%
Mali	10.5%
Ghana	10%

The East African Community (EAC) level

One of the fundamental principles of the East African Community is that it is people-driven, as provided for by Article 7 of the Treaty for the Establishment of the East African Community. Under this treaty, the partner states of Kenya, Tanzania and Uganda (joined by Rwanda and Burundi in 2007) set out a bold vision for their eventual unification. The vision of EAC is to have a prosperous, competitive, secure and politically united East Africa. The mission of EAC is to widen and deepen economic, political, social and cultural integration in order to improve the quality of life of the people of East Africa through increased competitiveness, value-added production, trade and investment.

In terms of leverage, this five-member bloc has a combined population of 111 million people, and a gross regional product (GRP) of some US$36,082 billion (all 2004 estimations) and a land mass of more than 1.8 million k^2 (cf. UNCTAD 2006; UN 2005; EAC 2006).

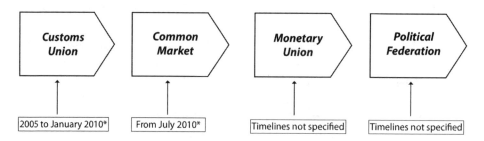

Figure 5.1: EAC integration stages and timelines.

Farmers' associations and their engagement with the EAC

A unique feature of the EAC (like the African Union), is that it grants observer status to CSOs in the region. However, a study commissioned by Kituo cha Katiba (Uganda) in 2009, which analysed (clause by clause) the rules for granting observer status for CSOs, revealed the need to restructure the rules for granting observer status.

Generally, observer status is granted by the Community itself, and it requires an organisation to attend the opening and closing sessions. A few organisations that have observer status in the EAC are: East African Business Council; East African Trade Union Council; East African Centre for Constitutional Development; East African Magistrates and Judges Association; East Africa Book Development Association; and East Africa Law Society (a CSO).

Associations that are on the waiting list for observer status are: International Council of Social Welfare; East African Youth Forum; Legal and Human Rights Centre (LHRC); East Africa Youth Forum (Kenya Chapter); East African Youth Development; East African Fine Coffees Association; Association of Professional Societies in East Africa; East African Confederation of Informal Sector Organisations; The Eastern African Sub-regional Support Initiative for the Advancement of Women.

Apart from the observer status, there is a civil society body that brings together CSOs from all over the EAC member countries. This newly-established organi-sation is called the East Africa Civil Society Forum – EACSOF – and is based in Arusha, Tanzania. This forum was formed to interface annually with the Summit of the EAC.

EAC and the implementation of the Maputo Declaration/CAADP protocol

All East African countries were represented at the Maputo meeting in 2003, with the exception of Uganda. However, by 2009, not one of the East African countries had realised their commitment to increase their budget allocation for agriculture and food security to 10 per cent.

In the financial year 2008/09, Tanzania's budget allocation for agriculture was 6 per cent, the same as Kenya's. In 2009/10, budget estimates show an increase in the agricultural sector of about 30 per cent for both Tanzania and Uganda. By 2009/10 it is estimated that Tanzania's budget allocations will reach 7.8 per cent, while Uganda will be about 4.9 per cent. Among the EAC member states, Rwanda is leading, and her budget estimate for 2009/10 is 9 per cent, close to the target. Kenya and Uganda continue to lag behind, while clear data for Burundi are unavailable. These statistics reveal the need for smallholder farmers to strategise and engage their governments by advocating and lobbying for the increased spending on agriculture and to ensure that funds are utilised properly to develop the agricultural sector and rural develop-ment in general.

Issues on agriculture and rural development in the EAC Development Strategy, 2006–2010

There are other instruments that could be used by farmer organisations to engage the sub-regional economic grouping. The East African Community operates on the basis of a five-year Development Strategy. The strategy document spells out the policy guidelines, priority programmes and implementation schedules.

EAC adopted a development strategy to facilitate the implementation of the Treaty in a systematic manner. The first EAC Development Strategy (1997–2000) was succeeded by the second EAC Development Strategy (2001–2005), which expired in December 2005. The third EAC Development Strategy was developed in 2006–2010. However, Rwanda and Burundi were not considered in this strategy, and efforts to find their strategic fit in a strategy that is already operational has been a challenge, hence the process to incorporate them is still in progress and could take some time.

The strategic interventions that have been proposed in this strategy have been driven by the following considerations: globalisation and intensification of competition in the global markets; emergence of other regional economic blocs; the links between regional and national plans and long-term visions; operationalising areas of common economic interests; consolidating peace and security in the region; setting the timeframe for various activities and proper sequencing; providing for an effective institutional mechanism to oversee implementation; greater involvement of the key stakeholders; empowering the citizens of East Africa to benefit from the EAC; marketing the community to the people of East Africa and the rest of the world; clarifying the roles of each organ of the EAC for the effective implementation of agreed policies and programmes to deliver tangible services and benefits; equitable sharing of benefits of the integration process, coupled with willingness to sacrifice by all stakeholders; enlargement of the EAC, and ensuring its sustainability.

The strategy focuses on the key pillars of East African integration. These are consolidating the implementation of the Customs Union, establishing a Common Market, and laying the foundations for a Monetary Union and a Political Federation.

EAC: Opportunities and challenges for smallholder farmers

Among the challenges for smallholder farmers are inadequate participation in the designing, implementation and review of the EAC development strategies. One reason for this is a lack of formal consultation mechanisms to involve stakeholders in EAC structures, despite the recognition of their role. A key principle of the strategy is participation of stakeholders in EAC affairs, but there is no clear mechanism for their involvement. However, the EAC, in collaboration with some stakeholders, such as the EAC Business Council, does organise annual forums. A visible shortcoming in these forums remains the inadequate representation of wider stakeholders, especially smallholder farmers.

Smallholder farmers and the Common Market for Eastern and Southern Africa (COMESA)

The Common Market for Eastern and Southern Africa (COMESA) was founded in 1993 as a successor to the Preferential Trade Area for Eastern and Southern Africa

(PTA), which was established in 1981. COMESA formally succeeded the PTA on 8 December 1994, upon ratification of the Treaty by 11 signatory states. The establishment of COMESA was a fulfilment of the requirements of the PTA Treaty, which provided for the transformation of the PTA into a common market ten years after the PTA Treaty.

In October 2000, substantial progress towards the eventual creation of a Customs Union was made with the announcement in Lusaka of the formation of a Free Trade Area (FTA). The member states of Djibouti, Egypt, Kenya, Madagascar, Malawi, Mauritius, Sudan, Zambia and Zimbabwe agreed to eliminate tariffs on goods which conform to the COMESA Rules of Origin.

The current member state of COMESA include Angola, Burundi, Comoros, the DRC, Djibouti, Egypt, Eritrea, Ethiopia, Kenya, Libya, Madagascar, Malawi, Mauritius, Rwanda, Seychelles, Sudan, Swaziland, Uganda, Zambia and Zimbabwe. The population of COMESA is estimated to be around 400 million, with an estimated GDP of around US$ 380 billion.

CAADP implementation within COMESA

COMESA has adopted the AU's approach to improving the agricultural sector under the CAADP, which calls for a 10 per cent budget allocation to this sector. This is hoped to improve the agricultural sector enough to reduce poverty by the year 2015. This programme at the COMESA secretariat is being handled by one of the technical committees on agriculture, which is responsible for the identification and implementation of regional programmes on agriculture.

In terms of dialogue procedure, the agricultural committee has a direct link with member state agricultural ministries and related institutions. Although there are no direct links between COMESA secretariat and smallholder farmers, organisations representing small-scale farmers in the region can easily be linked to the COMESA secretariat through the agricultural committee and the consultative committee of the business community, which is responsible for providing a link and facilitating dialogue between the business community and other interest groups and other organs of COMESA.

In terms of lobby and advocacy issues, smallholder farmer organisations should try to create a special desk under the agricultural committee to deal with problems affecting small-scale farmers in the region. In addition, farmer organisations should find their space on member state CAADP focal point committees which are cardinal in coming up with agriculture programmes with member states.

COMESA has made remarkable progress in CAADP implementation at the national level. By the end of 2009, 17 of the 19 member states had initiated the CAADP Round Table (RT) process. These were Rwanda, Malawi, Zambia, Kenya, Uganda, Ethiopia, Burundi, Seychelles, Djibouti, Madagascar, Zimbabwe, Sudan, Comoros, Egypt, Mauritius, Swaziland and the DRC. Of the 17 states, 12 have actually launched the CAADP RT process. In COMESA, the RT process is officially in place when the country appoints its focal-point person to begin the mobilisation of stakeholders. The big question is whether smallholder farmers are adequately aware and represented to the round tables.

The space for smallholder farmers in the COMESA agriculture programmes

Smallholder farmers form the majority of those involved in agricultural production. In terms of representation in the formulation of regional programmes, small-scale farmers are represented by the main agricultural organisations, such as Zambia National Farmers' Union (ZNFU) in the case of Zambia, and other agricultural agencies, such as Agriculture Consultative Forum (ACF). It is worth noting that farmer group representation is at member-state level and not directly at COMESA secretariat, whose role is to coordinate member-state programmes. All regional agricultural programmes are hinged on the Comprehensive Africa Agriculture Development Programme (CAADP).

Smallholder farmers and the Southern African Development Community (SADC)

The Southern African Development Community (SADC) has been in existence since 1980, when it was formed as a loose alliance of nine majority-ruled states in southern Africa, known as the Southern African Development Coordination Conference (SADCC), to coordinate development projects in order to lessen economic dependence on the then apartheid South Africa. The founding member states were Angola, Botswana, Lesotho, Malawi, Mozambique, Swaziland, United Republic of Tanzania, Zambia and Zimbabwe.

Currently, the SADC member states are Angola, Botswana, the DRC, Lesotho, Madagascar, Malawi, Mauritius, Mozambique, Namibia, Seychelles, South Africa, Swaziland, United Republic of Tanzania, Zambia and Zimbabwe. The secretariat of the SADC is based in Gaborone, Botswana.

The SADC vision is one of a common future within a regional community that will ensure economic well-being, the improvement of the standards of living and quality of life, freedom and social justice, and peace and security for the peoples of southern Africa. This shared vision is anchored on the common values and principles and the historical and cultural affinities that exist amongst the peoples of southern Africa.

SADC's agricultural sector

The agriculture sector features prominently in the SADC regional economy, contributing 35 per cent of its GDP. About 70 per cent of the population depends on agriculture for food, income and employment. Agriculture is also a major source of exports in several countries, contributing on average about 13 per cent to total export earnings and about 66 per cent to the value of intra-regional trade. For these reasons, the performance of agriculture has a strong influence on the rate of economic growth, the level of employment, demand for other goods, economic stability, food security and overall poverty reduction. However, the attainment of these goals is dependent on a trading environment that enables intra- as well as inter-regional trade to occur with minimal hindrance.

While the SADC region is well endowed with a diversified natural resource base, agricultural growth and productivity have been stagnant over the past twenty years. Agricultural incomes have declined and food insecurity has increased markedly. Poverty has increased, particularly in rural areas, thus accelerating a rural-urban migration. Unsustainable management techniques in agriculture and natural resources threaten the resource base itself.

There is a need to reverse the stagnation of the productivity of the sector and set SADC member states on the path of fast economic growth and poverty reduction. Halving severe poverty within the next 15 years – the stated goal of SADC heads of state – will require an average GDP growth of 8 per cent per annum over this period. This in turn will require agriculture to grow at an annual rate of more than 6 per cent over the same period. Achieving this very ambitious goal is not impossible. SADC's Regional Indicative Strategic Development Plan (RISDP) and the action plans from the SADC Extra-Ordinary Summit on Agriculture and Food Security (Dar-es-Salaam, 15 May 2004) provide a sound framework for achieving strong and sustained growth in agriculture and the overall rural economy. The plan stresses that the farmers' lack of access to agricultural inputs and markets are the major barriers to their development. Improving production systems, access to inputs and markets are therefore important missions of the Food Agriculture and Natural Resources (FANR) directorate.

Farmer-led organisations' participation in agriculture policy processes in southern Africa

The Southern African Confederation of Agricultural Unions (SACAU) has been earmarked by SADC as an organisation that represents the interests of the farmers in the region. On some occasions, SADC has used another NGO based in Gaborone as a convener of CSOs in the region. This organisation is called SADC CNGO. It is high time that SADC followed EAC and COMESA. COMESA as a regional organisation provides space for CSOs by entering into Memoranda of Understanding (MoU). On the other hand, COMESA and SADC can also copy a provision in clause 127 from the EAC, which provides CSOs with an opportunity to have observer status.

ESAFF's engagement

ESAFF is a farmer-initiated, farmer-lead and farmer-owned organisation. The origin of ESAFF is traced back to the Smallholder Farmers' Convergence (SFC), which was a parallel event at the World Summit on Sustainable Development (WSSD) held in Johannesburg, South Africa in August 2002.

The SFC was attended by more than 300 smallholder farmers from 19 countries representing Africa, Latin America, Canada, Europe and Asia. The purpose of this convergence was for smallholder farmers to have a forum to speak as a united voice so that their issues and recommendations could become an integral part of the deliberations and outcomes of the WSSD.

In a nutshell, ESAFF is a network of smallholder farmers that advocates for policy, practice and attitude change that reflects the needs, aspirations and development of small-scale farmers in eastern and southern Africa. In November 2009, ESAFF was active in 12 countries:

- Tanzania: National Network of Smallholder Farmers' Groups in Tanzania – MVIWATA;
- Kenya: Kenya Smallholder Farmers Forum – KESSFF;
- Uganda: ESAFF Uganda;
- Zambia: ESAFF Zambia;
- Zimbabwe: The Zimbabwe Movement of Small Organic Farmers – ZIMSOFF;
- Lesotho: Lesotho Smallholder Farmers' Forum,
- South Africa: South Africa Network of Smallholder Farmers' Forum – in Limpopo Province;
- Malawi: National Smallholder Farmers' Movement – NASFAM;
- Burundi: ESAFF Burundi;
- Rwanda: ESAFF Rwanda;
- Seychelles: Seychelles Farmers' Association – SEYFA; and
- Madagascar (CPM).

ESAFF's struggle for recognition and participation

The case of ESAFF Uganda – Community Action Planning

In Uganda, ESAFF district farmer leaders were involved in Community Action Planning (CAP) as way of adding the concerns and voices of smallholder farmers to the next budget cycle.

Before wider implementation, an example of CAP was carried out in Kisekende village so as to give the farmers a hands-on experience in CAP. Through CAP, citizens were able identify the most pressing issues facing them as farmers and suggest solutions to those issues. Farmers were aware of their roles and responsibility in shaping the local budget and were able to interface with some of the local leaders (sub-county chiefs and chairmen, parish chiefs), as well as the district planners, National Agricultural Advisory Services (NAADS) officer and the secretary for production.

Tanzania – social auditing and national agriculture budget analysis

Smallholder farmers in Tanzania implemented a project to enable them to participate in the Agriculture Strategic Development Programme (ASDP) in Mbozi,

Mbeya. The programme is indicative of a change in farmers' readinesss to participate in policy formulation practices in the district, and is evidenced by the fact
that project implementations in the district reflect the needs and expectations of
smallholder farmers. The project has enhanced accountability and transparency
– smallholder farmers now know their responsibility in policy formulation, participation and evaluation. At national level, smallholder farmers (through their
national network, MVIWATA) analyse the national annual budget and share their
opinions through the media and with Members of Parliament, thus influencing the
ongoing debate on agriculture financing.

ESAFF struggle for recognition and participation at national level: The case of ESAFF Zambia

ESAFF Zambia is working to engage grassroots communities and the Zambia
Parliamentary Committee (the Expanded Committee on Estimates) to ensure that
the needs and expectations of the smallholder farmers are reflected in the national
budget. They did this for the first time early in 2009. Some of the comments from
farmers were taken up by the government. For example, farmer involvement in the
distribution of fertiliser has improved the distribution significantly.

ESAFF Zambia submits comments on the annual agriculture budget and its
implementation to the Expanded Committee on Estimates. This includes comment
on how farmers benefited in the previous budget and proposals for improvement.

ESAFF's struggle for recognition and participation at regional level

ESAFF aknowledged that recognition and participation at grassroots and national
level is as important as it is at the regional and global levels. To achieve regional recognition, smallholder farmer leaders visited all three regional blocs between April
and June 2009: SADC in Gaborone, Botswana, COMESA in Lusaka, and the East
African Community headquarters in Arusha. The main objective was to explore
entry points for smallholder farmers to engage with the regional groupings.

ESAFF and COMESA

ESAFF representatives from Zambia visited COMESA and managed to establish
rapport with the organisation. A draft Memorandum of Understanding (MoU)
was developed and is still under review. The MoU has the objective of establishing
a framework of a formal working relationship between COMESA and ESAFF to
implement and promote regional initiatives in agriculture and engage in dialogue
on factors and policies that impact on agriculture.

ESAFF and SADC

ESAFF representatives from Zimbabwe visited SADC to explore the possibility of a
greater involvement in SADC issues regarding agriculture. The farmer leader met

the SADC officers responsible for agriculture, rural development and food security, as well as the director of livestock. However, it appears that there was some miscommunication between SADC headquarters ESAFF and nothing came of this. ESAFF is still struggling to establish this connection. As a new initiative, ESAFF is seeking to partner with SACAU, and with SADC CNGO, an NGO based in Botswana, to enable the voice of smallholder farmers to be heard within SADC.

ESAFF and EAC

Following a visit by a ESAFF representative to the East African Community (EAC) headquarters in Arusha, Tanzania, ESAFF was able to apply for observer status on the regional bloc. In additional, ESAFF is a member of the East African Civil Society Forum (EACSOF), which brings together all CSOs in the EAC who need to engage with the community.

Recommendations and conclusion

To attain full participation, the following factors should be in place:

- Strong smallholder farmers' organisations built up from grassroots to national level and sub-regional level. Proper structures and organisations would enable smallholder farmers to organise themselves, get correct information and have mechanisms to ensure consistent participation in policy processes at all levels. In the Eastern and Southern Africa (ESA) region, there are smallholder farmers' organisations in each country. However, most of these are in their infant stages so are weaker institutionally compared to the well-established commercial farmers' organisations. Since 2002, national smallholder farmers in the region have started to transform into strong institutions with a clear empowerment agenda. ESAFF, which is entirely smallholder farmer-initiated, -led and -owned, is struggling to mobilise and support the upcoming smallholder farmers' organisations in the ESA region.
- Proper mobilisation and organisation of smallholder farmers at all levels with proper infrastructure for communication, policy analyses and representation should be in existence.
- NGOs in the ESA region should work with smallholder farmers to mentor them and give them space to present their issues in policy dialogues.
- NGOs and smallholder farmers' organisations should forge working partnerships, share information and strategise together at all levels. These working relationship should be established at grassroots, national and regional levels. SACAU (in Southern Africa), EAFF (in Eastern Africa), PELUM Association as well as the farmer-led organisation, ESAFF, should forge working partnerships at sub-regional level.
- There is a need for the political will to open up channels of communication and participation from grassroots level, through national to sub-regional levels

(SADC, EAC and COMESA). Communication channels to enable smallholder farmers to participate in policy formulation and monitoring are still inadequate, partly due to a lack of organisation and understanding of the available opportunities. However, on the other hand, there is still no strong willingness to recognise and involve smallholder farmers in policy processes.

- Smallholder farmers require free access to user-friendly information on agriculture policies, declarations and budgets which they can easily understand, analyse and use for lobbying and advocating. Liaison offices should be established within local governments, national Parliaments, central governments, and at sub-regional level (SADC, EAC and COMESA). These liaison offices would act as entry points for smallholder farmers' organisations to get information to enable them to engage.

References

HakiElimu & Policy Forum (2008). *Understanding the Budget Process in Tanzania: A Civil Society Guide.*

Hakikazi Catalyst, REPOA & TGNP (2006). *Follow the Money.* www.repoa.or.tz

IFAD (2008). Report of the global meeting of the Farmers' Forum.

Oxfam, AfriMAP, An Open Society Institute (2009). *Strengthening Popular Participation in the African Union.*

The Foundation for Civil Society Tanzania (2006). Report of the CSOs exhibition to the Parliament.

Wilson, J. (2005). Understanding participation. In: T. Marange, M. Mukute & J. Woodend (eds). *Field Guide: Beyond Participatory Tools.*

World Bank (2008). World Development Report. *Agriculture for Development: An Overview.* Washington, DC: World Bank.

Stakeholder participation in the agricultural policy-making process: The case of Tanzania

Audax Rukonge

Background

A paradigm shift from socialism and a protectionist economy, and the demand for good governance practices in public office, has witnessed various types of collaboration among the three key players (that is, the public, private and civil society sectors) in development. Demand for egalitarian discourses and higher accountability standards underpin the current enthusiasm among these players for inclusivity and participatory, people-centred and sustainable policy processes. The process of engaging all the actors affected by interventions in all stages of policy-making is paramount to increasing ownership, empowerment and sustainability. It should be noted that participatory approaches must be espoused to ensure wider representation, and that marginal and vulnerable groups are part of the equation for good policy-making processes.

Stakeholders' groups in policy-making are not homogeneous and have widely varying demands, capabilities and interests. On the one hand, the magnitude, effort and level of coordination among actors is proportional to the effect of the policy and response by the government (that is, the higher the level of coordination and the greater the engagement, the more likely one is to get a positive response from the target audience). For this reason, stakeholder mapping is very important, and this should take into account the excluded, marginal and voiceless people in the society. Egalitarian discourses must seek to find ways to accommodate the voices of the 'unseen' stakeholders who ultimately bear the brunt of the negative outcomes resulting from decisions made by others.

Agricultural policy in Tanzania was spearheaded and underpinned by the short- and long-term national development trajectories as articulated in the National Development Vision and the National Strategy for the Growth and Reduction of Poverty (known by its Kiswahili acronym, MKUKUTA). The Tanzania Development Vision (TDV 2025) is an articulation of an enviable future, and envisages a substantially more developed society with a quality livelihood and well-educated people governed by better governance practices.

To realise this development vision, the national medium-term development plans were articulated in a five-year poverty-reduction strategy, MKUKUTA. The strategy has three main clusters that aim to reduce the proportion of people living below the poverty line, to improve quality of life and social wellbeing, and promote good governance and accountability. Apart from the medium-term development plans and national development vision, there are sectoral policies and strategies harmonised to respond to MKUKUTA goals and national development vision.

The sector policies, strategy and the national medium- and long-term strategies bring together a wide range of actors, including development partners (donors) and private and civil society sectors. At the higher level, the government has committed itself to promote democratic decision-making processes as a key principle of good governance. Tanzania follows a double approach, that is, the bottom-up and top-down policy/budget development mechanism. This approach provides opportunities for the duty bearers and rights holders to jointly and collaboratively assess their environment and set priorities based on their contexts.

This chapter examines the importance of stakeholder participation in agricultural policy-making processes at local, national and regional levels. It highlights the bottlenecks encountered in processes designed for stakeholder participation – drawing on the experience of Concern Tanzania's work at national and district levels. Briefly this chapter responds to the following key questions:

- What are the current models of stakeholder participation in agricultural policy-making process, and have these improved pro-poor policy outcomes?
- What are the most pressing constraints to effective farmer representation in agricultural policy formulation processes, and how can these be overcome?
- What is 'best practice' when designing models for smallholder farmer participation in policy-making at nation and regional levels?

Local context and planning process in the agricultural sector

The Tanzanian policy-making process recognises the vital role played by stakeholders at village, district and national levels. This recognition is based on the understanding that their participation can promote ownership and sustain desirable, productive and durable changes. Agricultural stakeholders are expected to engage, own and generate positive responses from the sector and to promote sustainability of interventions in order to overcome social injustices and inequalities, and to address poverty.

The government and 'development partners' (donors) are supporting the Agriculture Sector Development Programme (ASDP) through a basket fund. The district councils (DCs) utilise this grant system through the District Agricultural Development Plans (DADPs), which provides services to citizens in line with the priorities identified by their communities. Beyond the government and donors, civil society organisations (CSOs) and other private organisations work at the community level in similar activities to DCs, and are perceived to be important stakeholders in the agricultural sector.

Decentralisation aims at giving power to local institutions and communities – especially the rural poor – to prioritise their development interventions and mobilise resources. With support from DCs and the national government, villages form

Village Agricultural Development Plans (VADPs) through participatory approaches and based on extensive village consultation. Under the chairmanship of the ward councillors, the VADPs are reviewed and are assessed before submission to district level.

However, although DADPs are overarching sectoral plans for agricultural activities in the districts, DCs and CSOs may follow plans separate from each other. Coordination is vital, but the agricultural departments in the districts are challenged during priority setting, planning, and implementation and monitoring of the DADPs. The financial resources from CSOs are neither captured nor reflected in district plans, despite the substantial contribution from the civil society sector working in agriculture in Tanzania. The ward-level compilation process of villages' priorities often engage the DADP facilitation teams and technical individuals at the ward level without involving CSOs in the process at all. CSOs use the project implementation approach and, depending on the origin of the funding, their planning season, reporting format, and time might be different from that of the local government.

Despite the measures to involve stakeholders, smallholder farmers face misrepresentation, exclusion and low budgetary allocation to address their specific demands. Due to low resources and problems in decentralisation, because of the centralised planning culture that doesn't include smallholder farmers, it is evident that smallholders' priorities are overlooked and curtailed by the socioeconomic and political environments. One example is the access to information that farmers can understand. Usually policies are in English and only the summary or popular versions are produced in the Kiswahili language for villagers.

Models of stakeholder participation in agricultural budget and policy-making processes

There are two models of involving stakeholders in policy-making processes in Tanzania. The local and national level processes have different dimensions which are linked to address the national and local priorities necessary to achieve the national development goals. The local-level model is represented in Figure 6.1, while the national-level model is articulated in Figure 6.2. Figure 6.1 indicates how the plans are generated from local (village level) to the national level. At local level, through participatory techniques, the planning/budgeting process captures priorities articulated by smallholder and marginal farmers, farmers' unions, cooperatives and associations.

The Opportunities and Obstacles for Development (O&OD) approach is intended to enhance inclusivity and to empower citizens to monitor the implementation process and demand increased accountability.

The first planning unit is at the village level. In the village assembly meetings and during the Ward Facilitation Teams' consultations with smallholder farmers, CSOs and other actors are expected to give their input into the process. At the district

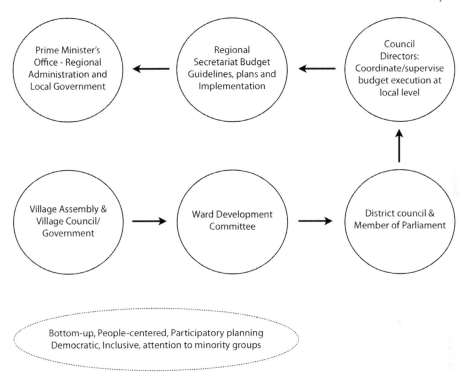

Figure 6.1: Local government planning process

council level, ward councillors and Members of Parliament approve the district sector comprehensive plans. Plans and budgets by non-state actors (NSAs) are expected to be reflected in the village and district level plans. Plans from districts are expected to have gone through a bottom-up and participatory approach which promotes downward accountability. The regional secretariats review districts plans based on national priorities and budget guidelines before the plans are submitted to the national level for compilation.

Although there is a model for stakeholder participation that provides opportunities for the poor and marginal farmers to engage constructively in budget and policy processes, many challenges remain. These local level challenges include:

- Limited coordination of agricultural activities at the local level;
- Weak capacity and poor coordination amongst farmers;
- Blind agricultural policies that assume that farmers' groups are homogeneous;
- Low level of stakeholder participation and duplication of activities and interventions among actors
- Weak links between farmers and support institutions such as research, financial and private institutions;
- Production-oriented planning vis-à-vis market-oriented plans that put emphasis on value chain and technological improvement.

The national-level planning process is managed by the Ministry of Finance and Economic Affairs (MoFEA). Through the budget and guidelines committee, the MoFEA supports ministries and development agencies (MDAs) by providing guidelines and expenditure limits. Figure 6.2 defines the budget cycle process, through which MDAs and district councils are expected to plan based on a three-year rolling plan approach, that is, the Medium-term Expenditure Framework (MTEF). National-level stakeholders (such as farmers' umbrella organisations, NGOs, private companies, parliamentary committee on agriculture, livestock and water, donors, research institutions) can also influence the budget/policy on agriculture in various forums, such as sector performance reviews and parliamentary sector meetings before the parliamentary budget deliberations.

Every December, the MoFEA and the Prime Minister's Office – Regional Administration and Local Government (PMO-RALG) generate budget ceilings (Indicative Planning Figures or IPFs) and guidelines for the following fiscal year. The guidelines reflect the ASDP and Agricultural Sector Development Strategy (ASDS) priorities as well as MKUKUTA and TDV 2025. The IPFs and budget guidelines are shared with local government authorities (LGAs), ministries, departments and agencies before plans and allocations are made at village, district, regional and department levels.

Coordination of stakeholders' activities

There is a significant duplication of efforts from CSOs in identifying needs of villagers. This duplication has implications in terms of resources, time, consultation fatigue and unmet expectations among the community. One major limitation for joint plans and implementation processes at local level is the lack of CSO sector profile and coordination at the district level. District Agricultural and Livestock Officers (DALDOs) have little knowledge of organisations working in their areas, and there are no requirements for stakeholder mapping. Therefore CSOs rarely subscribe to DADPs, and plan their own activities that are not necessarily reflected in district documents. This scenario is contrary to ASDP and DADP guidelines and the DADP reporting format, in which it is mandatory for the DCs to report on budgets and activities executed by other service providers in the sector.

While the government articulates the role of private service providers in delivery of ASDP, CSOs (both local and international) have not been aggressive in tapping such opportunities to influence plans and budgets, or better practices for service delivery. Although there is an increased call for sector coordination at both local and national level to harmonise efforts and pool resources, CSOs and private companies maintain a parallel process that ends up duplicating activities. It will be difficult to coordinate such activities in the district unless:

- Stakeholder profiles are established and updated on a regular basis;
- Forums are forged that bring stakeholders together at least twice a year.

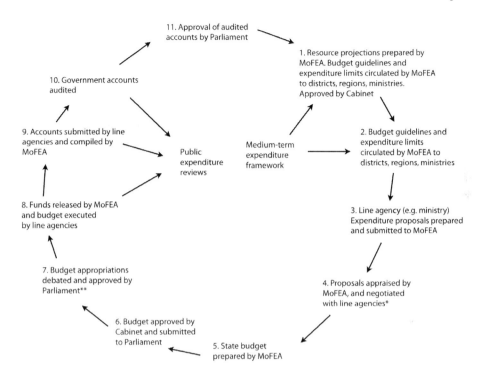

Figure 6.2: The budget cycle

* Negotiations are critical to budget allocations.

** Budget debate and approval often superficial and done in haste.

Adapted from Hakikazi Catalyst. Demystifying the budget process in Tanzania. A seminar to promote civil society advocacy.

There have been some attempts by DCs to designate a particular location (ward, village, division) to member CSOs with neither a collaborative strategy nor support mechanism in place, and there have been some initiatives to invite CSOs at compilation stage to form the DADPs. This is a commendable step towards a collaborative approach. However, the time for consultation and the level of participation is still limited. It has led to certain villages or wards receiving a high level of support, and others none at all. There is also an issue of political interests hampering the fair distribution of support to poor villages. Civil servants at both ward and district levels concede that in many cases priorities are compromised as they succumb to political pressure. Ward councillors in some districts insist that 'their farmers' get allocations of the DADP grants. Decisions based on such pressure at times jeopardise professionalism and can sacrifice strategic investments aimed at benefiting the whole district.

The national-level policy dialogue is based on Figure 6.2. Donor support is based on agreed principles in line with the Paris Declaration on aid. Despite this, however, chances are high that donors, who contribute significantly to the agricultural sector, might influence the agenda – a case of whoever pays the piper selects the tune! The agricultural budget, especially the development component, depends on development partners' contributions, despite the general budget support. Actually the level of engagement between donors and government is very advanced compared to other domestic non-state actors, especially the civil society and private sector organisations. Non-state actors can, however, influence the government and pro-poor policy actions through analytical policy briefs that are well researched and articulated with solid recommendations.

It should be noted that, at national level, non-state actors do not reflect similar agendas and priorities. For instance, if agri-business companies are lobbying for reduced export tax for agricultural produce and tax exemption for agricultural tools, mechanisms have to be developed to ensure farmers are benefiting from such waivers. Likewise, if private companies and big estate owners are lobbying for subsidised inputs (tractors, fertilisers and other agro-chemicals), smallholder farmers' umbrella organisations and CSOs have to ensure that the priorities, needs and rights of the majority are honoured and protected. Unfortunately this is not a simple decision. Strategic thinking has to be applied.

In Tanzania, non-state actors (including smallholder farmers' umbrella organisations such as MVIWATA)[1] participate in policy dialogue at national level. Farmers' umbrella involvement at national level is challenged by vicinity, proximity and capacity. Limited coordination at local level translates into varying signals on what farmers' needs are at national level. Likewise, farmers' associations are recovering from a negative legacy of poor cooperation and performance in the past, and few smallholders subscribe to farming associations. Despite the decentralised governance system, most policy decisions are made at national level, and this calls for better coordination and coherence. The Agriculture Non-State Actors' Forum (ANSAF) in Tanzania is such an institution, formed by individual member organisations involving civil society and private companies to harness their experience in the sector and advise donors and government accordingly.

Working within the guidelines

Although the NGO Code of Conduct and NGO Act both require NGOs to be transparent and accountable, information gathered with regard to budget sharing, participatory planning and accountability indicates that very few NGOs are abiding by the rules and promoting transparent practices in their programme operations. For example, the following problems are encountered:

- There is limited engagement and a reluctance to share quarterly reports and annual plans. Those who do produce reports and plans submit the information only to the relevant offices;

---

[1] MVIWATA is a smallholder farmers' organisation that advocates for pro-poor farmers' policies and practices. It has membership throughout the country and government recognises its importance in the agricultural sector.

- There is poor feedback from both sides;
- CSOs' budgets are not widely shared;
- Narrative and financial reports with downward accountability are largely absent;
- CSOs and community-based organisations (CBOs) are contracted by DCs without proper contract procedures, and there is limited follow up by ward-level extension agents, which puts public money in jeopardy.

With improved checks and balances in place, NGOs entrusted with public resources are expected to operate more ethically, thereby promoting accountability and transparency in financial matters. But multi-accountability levels (department heads and district heads) make accountability very difficult, unless the various stakeholders within the district agree to establish basic standards. There is no structure in place to monitor compliance, and within the complexities of the civil service structure it is difficult to agree on standards. For instance, in some districts the practice is for reports to be submitted to the district commissioners' and district executive directors' reception offices. Other districts submit their reports to the planning officer or the community development officer (CDO). This approach has two implications:

- It might take time before the CDO informs the DALDO on issues that need immediate action/attention;
- It could weaken sector coordination at local level.

Pooling resources and level of stakeholder participation

The operations undertaken by CSOs at local level consume a substantial amount of resources, and finances in particular. National and international NGOs are involved in service delivery at district, ward and village levels. These actors come into DADPs as private service providers, mobilisers, technical advisers and resource providers. This means CSOs and other private organisations bring in human, capital and financial resources at the local level. But how many of these resources complement those under the district agriculture development grant system? This is not well documented and could spell resource misallocation, resulting in very little impact on food security and poverty alleviation initiatives. It is therefore imperative that stakeholder mapping should seek to improve quality of DADP plans through efficient resource allocation.

Table 6.1: DADP grants for the first three quarters of 2008/09

District	Government (TShs)	CSOs (TShs)
Kasulu	382,245,419	178,700,000
Kibondo	282,689,235	349,765,015
Kigoma D.C.	296,280,988	229,334,992

Table 6.1 presents an example from the Kigoma region in Tanzania, indicating the level of financial contribution from CSOs working in the region, and transfers from central government to support DADP-related activities. Based on the data available from the prime minister's office, funds transferred to DCs for the first three quarters of the 2008/09 fiscal year indicate that Kasulu district council received a greater allocation from government than other districts.

A recent survey, conducted by Concern Tanzania for CSOs working in the Kigoma region, indicated that non-state actors are key in pushing agricultural agendas at the local level as well. The results showed that Kibondo district received significantly more from CSOs than it did from government, whereas in the Kasulu district, government contributed almost twice as much as CSOs, while in Kigoma district a substantial amount was availed by CSOs.

This documents government and CSO funding but, in addition, the private sector will have further information on the resources they do, or would be prepared to, invest in these districts. In most cases, CSOs and private institutions have supported the agricultural sector at local level through parallel initiatives. For instance in Iringa[2] there are financial institutions which offer financial support as soft loans to invest in agricultural related activities, but few of these have their activities coordinated by LGAs.

At the district level, CSOs and other private organisations have been criticised for not contributing enough resources to DADP implementation. In most of the areas in which Concern Tanzania works this is not accurate. In Iringa,[3] Kilolo and Masasi,[4] CSOs contribute sizable amounts of money to agricultural activities. Iringa receives more funds from CSOs and private organisations for agricultural-related activities than it does from government. However, Concern Tanzania's experience indicates that CSOs also have other resources, such as transport, access to information (especially internet facilities), and expertise in fields such as participatory planning approaches and community mobilisation. Local authorities are not utilising these resources, and they are rarely considered.

Improvement in pro-poor policy outcomes

Discussion on pro-poor policy outcomes can be made based on allocative and operational efficiency by looking at budget and national priorities. The national agricultural budget share going to local level has been little above 50% (see Table 6.2). Based on the understanding that meaningful interventions are taking place at local level, there is a need to increase allocation of the budget to local level.

---

[2]   Iringa financial data not included here.

[3]   CSOs in Iringa include Concern, TAGRODE, ACT-TAP, Anglican Church, SHILDA, Caritas – Iringa, and private organisations/NGOs offering financial loans include PRIDE, Dunduliza and Hugo van Lawick.

[4]   CSOs in Masasi district include KIMAS, MAFAMA, Dutch Connection, MAWODEA, Anglican MERESA, MECAA, and ROSDO.

Table 6.2: DADP Fund transfers (in million Tshs) 2006/07–2008/09[5]

DADG	CBG	EBG	DIDF	Grand Total	Year
9,154	3,293	1,566	165	14,178	2006/07
25,118	15,484	9,012	7,386	57,000	2007/08
17,453	17,984	18,812	4,635	58,885	2008/09

Source: PMO-RALG, 2009

The local level allocations are based on the three important sub-components of grant system.[6] Over the period of three years, the investment (DADG) component received a substantial amount of funds. Strangely enough, the 2008/09 allocations for the three major sub-components was almost the same, with the EBG receiving the most funding. In analysing the allocative efficiency, one is tempted to find out where the money is actually being spent for each category.

Figure 6.3[7] shows the levels of spending per priority under the investment (DADG) component. This component receives about 60 per cent of the local budget and it is expected to cover strategic investment that may trigger development activities in the rural areas.

Although the trends indicate substantial funds being transferred to LGAs, allocations at district levels have gone to irrigation and farmer training. Funds going to farmer training, strengthening farmer field schools and demonstration plot interventions should result in changed agricultural practices, improved technology, production and productivity that could lead to improved livelihoods, thereby empowering smallholder producers. Unfortunately this analysis does not inform the reader on changed attitudes and production practices based on such training.

Funds going to irrigation activities, animal health and crop market infrastructure improvements are substantial. These are among strategic investments in the sector. However, in order to improve pro-poor policy outcomes and to transform agriculture and smallholder farmers into business entities, consideration should be given to farm implements as well.

At the sub-regional and regional levels, countries should be able to live up to their commitments and hold each other accountable. However, given the limited

---

[5] For the 2008/09 transfers, the only information available on funds released was for the first three quarters.

[6] The local-level agricultural grant system includes the basic district agricultural development grant (DADG), capacity building grant (CBG) and extension block grant (EBG). The district irrigation development fund (DITF) is based on a competitive basis and opportunities available – especially water sources for irrigation.

[7] Source: IDASA-ANSAF Budget Tracking and Smallholder Agriculture Project baseline data for Tanzania.

engagement of CSOs and weak coordination among non-state actors, the chances are limited that smallholder priorities will be taken into account, unless politically influenced.

Therefore when designing models for smallholder farmer participation at national and regional platforms farmers umbrella organisations should be encouraged to raise their voices and create pressure at all levels. The Maputo Declaration and CAADP both focus on targets for smallholder farmers and agriculture in particular. Such commitments are not necessarily owned or even known by the local people. With this in mind, regional commitments can be achieved if would-be stakeholders are well informed and actively engaged through civil societies and other mechanisms of representation.

As the above analysis reveals, there are a number of challenges which are preventing stakeholders from participating fully at both local and national levels:

- Complexity of the agricultural sector stakeholders: Large private companies, farmers associations and CSOs all have varying demands, as do smallholder, medium and large-scale farmers with their varying needs. This calls for tailor-made support to such groups, to ensure that they all benefit from available public resources. Furthermore, an increased emphasis on contract farming and pushing the private sector as an engine for economic growth, needs to take into account the implications of change for smallholder farmers.

- Donors contribution to the sector through basket funds and general budget support: development partners contribute a significant amount to the agricultural sector. Accountability can be promoted through open dialogue. However if most of the development partners pull out of the sector, on-going activities will be affected. Currently most CSOs find it difficult to access information directly from the government or donors.

- Lack of a strong legitimate national body capable of raising farmers' concerns: Dar es Salaam remains the centre for strategic engagement on national policy. Organised engagement demands continuous presence in various decision-making forums, which is difficult when these take place in Dar es Salaam. At local level, most of farmers' organisations are still weak and farmers are reluctant to join cooperative societies.

- Lack of transparency and access to information at local level: Tanzania's constitution recognises the right to information, however, experience reveals difficulty in getting relevant documentation from government. Although there are attempts by some LGAs to display income and expenditures on notice boards, analysis points to issues of language being an impediment to quality information.

- Mindset and status-quo among some civil servants: changing the status quo is always a challenge for movers and shakers of agricultural sector transformation. Changes within the government system will always take time, but what is important is the involvement of stakeholders in designing the routes for change.

Conclusion

In Tanzania there are good models to ensure smallholder and stakeholder participation in agricultural policy processes. Smallholder farmers will continue to lead agricultural production for both food and non-food export[8] crops in Tanzania. The model provided under Opportunities and Obstacles for Development (O & OD), the local planning process, as well as the national budget provide avenues within which stakeholders can engage constructively. However there is little understanding and clarity among farmers, CSOs and the private sector of what takes place, when and where, so stakeholders engage in myriad activities. In order for DADPs to deliver ASDP and transform agriculture, a certain degree of coordination has to be adopted by stakeholders at both local and national levels. Regional engagement can be coordinated through intra- and inter-regional forums that put smallholder farmers in decision-making forums at all levels.

Similarly the role of private service providers, including CSOs, should be central in delivering DADPs in terms of expertise and other resources contributed at district level. The presence of other actors beyond the government and development partners can be better harnessed through:

- Stakeholder mapping of agricultural service providers is essential at all levels of planning and decision-making so as to highlight technical and support services.
- To increase ownership, transparency and accountability (vertical and horizontal) and avoid duplication of activities there is a need for CSOs to undertake internal self-reflection. This should lead to increased citizen involvement in village plans – working with public officials during the planning season. CSO participation at village level should mean that smallholder farmers' priorities and needs are articulated.
- Local, national and regional sectoral forums will encourage collaboration, strengthen the coordination role of the public sector, and reduce monitoring costs. This approach will strengthen the supervisory role played by local councillors and Members of Parliament, and increase accountability from government and non-state actors.

There is an urgent need for a paradigm shift from rhetoric to reality, to embrace participatory and egalitarian discourses among actors in the various sectors. This will encourage trust and joint interventions for sector performance, food security and reduced poverty.

The traditional approach to the planning process involved government officials alone, and now needs to be replaced with a joint planning approach at the district level. CSOs will be expected to deliver services and perform other duties, including knowledge brokering for better policy implementation. CSOs and other private organisations need to come together, work with the government, be transparent, and be practical about implementation, and adjust plans to meet local needs. This

---

[8]   This is the case for cashew nut, coffee and cotton production, where a large share of exports is produced by smallholder farmers.

kind of collaboration and flexibility will go further than the current system to ensure that poor farmers receive the services they need and deserve.

References

Concern Tanzania (2009). The role of private service providers in delivering DADPs in Tanzania. Unpublished paper.

HAKIKAZI Catalyst (2005). Demystifying the budget process in Tanzania. A seminar to promote civil society advocacy.

URT (2006). District Agricultural Development Plans (DADP): Guidelines.

URT (2005). Medium-term Expenditure Framework.

URT (2005). Mkakati wa Kukuza Uchumi na Kuondoa Umasikini Tanzania (MKUKUTA) or National Strategy for Growth and Reduction of Poverty in Tanzania.

URT (1998). Tanzania Development Vision 2025.

URT (2008). Prime Minister's Office Regional Administration and Local Government: Budget and Releases of DADP Funds.

URT (2009). Ministry of Agriculture and Food Security: The Agricultural Budget Share of the National Budget (2006–2009).

URT (2009). DADP Local Government Transfers 2006/07– 2008/09).

Enhancing smallholder farmers' policy engagement with policy through southern African farmers' organisations

Benito Eliasi, Stéphanie Aubin and Ishmael Sunga

Introduction

Agriculture remains the mainstay of most economies in African countries. It provides employment to more than 60 per cent of the population and accounts for about one third of the continent's GDP. It also plays an important role in addressing food insecurity and poverty challenges. The 2008 World Development Report (WDR) of the World Bank stated that growth in GDP attributable to agriculture is at least twice as important in reducing poverty as non-agricultural sectors. Besides, the recent food price crisis has highlighted the critical importance of targeting food self-sufficiency. Given that most production (especially staples) comes from small-scale and low-income farmers, these are particularly well positioned to assist with this endeavour. Moreover, as the agricultural sector has important backward and forward linkages with other sectors, agricultural growth has a potentially high multiplier effect on the rest of the economy. Although small-scale farming plays a very critical role in agricultural production, smallholder farmers' involvement in the development of agricultural policies and programmes has been minimal, which has resulted in agricultural interventions which are, in most cases, ineffective. The challenge emanates from the policy-makers who have not fully embraced the concept of farmers' participation, as well as weaknesses within farmers' representative structures (farmers' organisations).

The role of agriculture in Africa

In the short and medium term, agriculture is likely to keep its central role in African economies, considering the fact that no other sector seems to be in a position to absorb the much higher rural population growth prevailing on the continent. Unlike in East Asia and the Pacific region, where there has been an observed decline in the number of rural poor (most of which depend on agriculture for livelihood), in South Asia and sub-Saharan Africa the number of rural poor has continued to rise and will likely exceed the number of urban poor until 2040. Projections in Africa indicate that the population will double by 2050 to 1.7 billion. This will translate into huge pressure in terms of feeding and sustaining the livelihoods of this growing population.

Beyond Africa's challenge to satisfy the agricultural needs, both in terms of food and energy for the growing global population, there are other emerging issues, such as natural disasters, the recent food price crisis and climate change impact projections, that have to be addressed by African farmers. Agriculture is again one of the world's top priorities, as demonstrated by renewed international interest in it over the past decade. The first Millennium Development Goal (MDG) to halve poverty and hunger before 2015 is clearly agriculture-related as 70 per cent of the world's poor live in rural areas and rely on agriculture as a livelihood. The WDR 2008, entitled *Agriculture for Development*, provided another momentum for a new focus and a new perspective on agriculture by strongly restating it as a main sector of economic activity in most developing countries. In spite of the very volatile global environment, the international community is re-engaging with coordinated efforts (for example, the UN high level task force launched in April 2008) and new commitments (such as the pledge made by the G8 countries at their July 2009 meeting to mobilise US\$ 20 billion to boost food security in developing countries). Furthermore, there has been the emergence of new participants in worldwide philanthropy (notably the Bill and Melinda Gates Foundation) in promoting agriculture alongside health as important areas of support to the poorest countries. As far as African governments are concerned, the strategic role of agriculture has been permanently reaffirmed through the development and implementation of the NEPAD Comprehensive African Agriculture Development Programme (CAADP) and the Maputo Declaration to devote 10 per cent of the annual national budget to the agricultural sector, to achieve agricultural growth of 6 per cent by 2015.

Looking at the past, however, although billions of US dollars have been invested in agriculture in Africa since the independence period, Africa has become a permanent food importer, agricultural productivity has decreased, poverty and hunger have increased and migration to cities and emigration have been exacerbated. This is happening despite the fact that vast land areas with agricultural potential are still unexploited (FAO, 2009) and large areas of exploited land could still be upgraded, notably through irrigation and enhanced inputs utilisation, to improve their productivity.[1] It is critical that the new commitments made in favour of African agriculture are optimised by learning from past experiences in order to reverse this situation and unlock the potential of African agriculture.

One of the reasons for the past failures encountered in the support of African agriculture lies in the top-down nature that characterised the policy-making and implementation processes. These rarely included effective consultations with farmers, particularly smallholder farmers, despite the fact that they constitute the majority of stakeholders. As 'end-users' of agricultural policies, smallholder farmers are best placed to provide relevant inputs in the policy formulation and monitoring processes. However, for their contributions to be effective, it is important that they

---

[1]   According to the FAO brief, only 3% of food crop land is under irrigation on the African continent, against 20% worldwide. Input utilisation only reaches 13 kg/ha input, against 73 kg in the Middle-East and 190 kg in South-East Asia.

speak with one legitimate and recognised voice. They also need to have appropriate policy development and advocacy capacities. This chapter argues that both can be performed by professional farmers' organisations that are well structured, representative, well governed, accountable and well capacitated.

The policy-making environment in the agricultural sector in sub-Saharan Africa: A complex landscape

The *raison d'être* of policies is to realise the concrete implementation of political commitments towards goals, objectives and strategies decided by leaders. Policies are ideally aimed at ensuring an enabling operating environment for the various players to be able to undertake their respective responsibilities towards the set goals. In the public domain, it is the responsibility of public authorities to determine appropriate 'rules of the game' that will fulfil these functions. In particular, it can only be public decision-making institutions, be they at global, continental, regional, national or local levels, that can establish and maintain the fundamental conditions of macroeconomic stability, political stability, security and rule of law, which are a prerequisite for the viable and sustainable development of the society. Public policies, however, may be initiated either from within or outside the realm of the public sector.

Creating public policies is a complex undertaking that requires balancing and harmonising the needs and aspirations of various actors and stakeholders whose expectations might be divergent. Given the central role of African agriculture in poverty alleviation and economic transition, the formulation and implementation of agricultural policies is all the more complex since they must be carefully coordinated with those of other sectors and must deal with different scales. In the globalised world, there is also a need to ensure compatibility with various international commitments and constraints, which adds another layer of complexity. Sometimes development partners have other requirements that have to be considered when formulating policies. These have to be balanced with local requirements to avoid policies that address donor requirements rather than local needs.

For decades in Africa, public institutions regarded policy-making as their sole domain. Extensive consultation with all the players concerned, particularly the end-users, was minimal. The trend has changed recently, mainly due to new practices promoted by the international development community, coupled with the realisation by African governments that policies that are formulated without consultation succeed rarely in addressing the targeted challenges. For example, the Cotonou Economic Partnership Agreement negotiations made the participation of non-state actors mandatory, which compelled government negotiators to involve the other actors in the process (including farmers). Likewise, within the framework of the formulation of the SADC Regional Agricultural Policy (RAP), consultation with all stakeholders in the agricultural sector, including farmers, was a requirement given to the consultant conducting the exercise. Civil society organisations (CSOs) and researchers in particular have emphasised the importance of multi-stakeholder approaches to ensure ownership and demand-driven processes as sound bases for any sustainable development initiative. Recent initiatives of devolution and decentralisation are also mechanisms that are making popular participation in policy formulation more and more systematic.

Although policy-making and review processes in Africa have become more open to different players, much still needs to be done if effective participation of smallholder farmers is to be fully realised across the board. The southern African policy-making landscape abounds with examples of farmers still not involved in the agricultural policy processes. For example, in the area of standard-setting processes for agriculture production and marketing, up until recently there was no structure for dialogue and consultation between the public institutions and the private sector, including producers, yet they were expected to apply these standards in the region (SACAU-DFID, 2008). Another illustration is provided within the framework of the implementation of the Aid for Trade agenda, a 2005 initiative of the World Trade Organisation. Aimed at providing additional aid funding for fostering trade as a growth and development engine, Aid for Trade is crucial for the agricultural sector in southern Africa. One of the elements of the initiative was to constitute national committees comprising recipient country governments, donors and other relevant stakeholders such as the private sector, in order to ensure that resources match needs, including in the agricultural sector. The reality is that such committees still do not exist in most southern Africa countries (SACAU, 2008). On the international scene, the fact that there are no representatives of African smallholder farmers in the food aid committee of the Food Aid Convention, even though food aid has major impacts on their production, demonstrates this further.

Besides this, when consultations are eventually implemented by public authorities, their effectiveness is often weakened by inappropriate timing. Participants either join in too early or too late to have any real impact. Figure 7.1 depicts the comparative chances of influencing policy-makers at the different stages of the policy-formulation process.

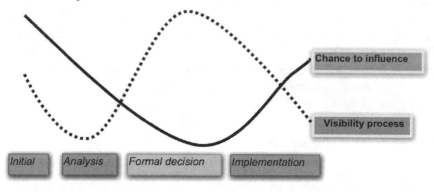

Figure 7.1: The decision-making process and chance to influence the outcome.

Source: SACAU Lobby Guide: 42

In general terms, the policy-making process goes through four broad phases, as depicted in the diagram. Activities under the initial phase are, in most cases, invisible to the public. Ironically, this is the phase at which policy-makers consult with various stakeholders for them to thoroughly understand the issues and elements to be addressed in the policy under development. Chances of influence are higher in this initial phase than in any other phase. The process becomes more visible to people in later phases, and, unfortunately, the more the process becomes visible the more difficult it becomes to influence the outcome. In most cases these are the stages at which most stakeholders join the process. The least chance of influencing the outcome is in the formal decision-making phase, when much thought, time and money have already gone into the decision; hence it becomes almost impossible to convince the decision-makers to take other views into account. Yet, it is often just before a policy is presented to the last executive level that farmers' representatives are consulted. In these conditions, consultations seek endorsement rather than concrete contributions. The recent case of the Zambian CAADP compact gives a good illustration of this propensity of government to consult farmers only for formality's sake. Within the CAADP framework, consultations with stakeholders are compulsory. However, the Zambian farmers were consulted at the very last stage of the compact formulation process[2] to give their endorsement to the document before presentation to government for final signature. In protestation against this *fait accompli*, the Zambian National Farmers' Union (ZNFU) refused to endorse the document and requested to be given the necessary time to undertake a thorough analysis of it and to provide their input. As a result, the signing of the endorsed document was delayed for several months until farmers gave their inputs.

Figure 7.1 also illustrates that the chance to influence increases again in the implementation phase. Indeed, the changing operational environment might necessitate adaptations or revisions, and the decision-makers will be searching for alternatives. It is important that farmers are also involved in the monitoring and review processes of policy implementation. Again, this feature rarely happens in the policy landscape of southern Africa.

The absence of African smallholder farmers in policy-making processes is notable at national, regional and continental and levels. While smallholder farmers represent about two thirds of the continent's population and have significant economic weight, the fact that policy-makers can still afford to ignore them poses questions.

Why should smallholder farmers be involved in policy processes?

Smallholder farmers are generally defined in terms of the size of land holdings, but this could vary by type of farm commodity. African smallholders are also often

---

[2] A compact is a signed document containing agricultural investment areas for a country or a region. The development of the document is part of the CAADP process and key stakeholders in a country or the region are signatories to the document.

associated with the limited scale of farming, which is characterised by a main orientation towards subsistence, dependence on family labour for most activities, and operation in resource-poor conditions. These conditions include low utilisation of purchased inputs, low access to technology, limited resources in terms of capital, skills and risk management, and limited capacity in terms of marketing, storage and processing (Syngeta Foundation, 2009). More than half of the African population amongst the poorest depends on the smallholding agricultural sector for their livelihoods; moreover, smallholder farmers produce the bulk of the continent's food supply and significantly contribute to African economies through employment and GDP (FAO, 2009). Thus the poor conditions in which African smallholder farmers operate represent a major constraint, not only for the livelihoods of the majority of Africans, but also for the contribution of the sector to national/regional food security and economic growth.

Given the current low productivity levels that are prevailing in the smallholder sector, as well as the significant amount of additional land that could be exploited for agricultural purposes on the continent, the development potential of the African smallholder sector is significantly huge (FAO, 2009). Nevertheless to unleash this potential, there is a need for policy-makers to ensure that smallholder farmers fully participate in the policy-making processes. In many instances policy-makers have failed to understand the complexity of the environment under which these farmers operate, which has often led to poor policies. Due to natural factors of endowment, the characteristics of the agrarian systems in Africa, related distribution of assets among rural households, and the type of linkages to markets are indeed hetero-geneous. The situation of smallholder farmers in terms of availability and access to appropriate enhancing technologies is also very diverse across the continent. This leads to different configurations of opportunities and constraints, and hence requires targeted approaches and tailor-made policy design. As recently emphasised by FAO, these required specific solutions can only derive through participatory pro-cesses (FAO, 2009). Consultation is also key for ownership, which is a determining factor of later commitment to implementation. A two-way dialogue therefore needs to be established between smallholder farmers and the other players responsible for determining the political, economic, legal as well as technological framework within which farmers operate. This also applies to policy issued by private sector operators, which have an impact on farming production (such as supermarkets, input suppliers and food processors).

It is also essential that smallholder farmers are involved in the policy processes of the other sectors that are linked to agriculture. Furthermore, the multiple and interlinked layers of policy engagement imply that smallholder farmers have to be involved at all levels of policy formulation and implementation.

The challenge is how to effectively engage with smallholder farmers and how to provide the appropriate support to enable them to organise effectively at all levels in order to be genuinely represented.

Challenges facing smallholder farmers in their participation in policy processes

Absence or minimal participation of southern African smallholder farmers in policy process originates from various factors, which can either be internal or external. The following sections outline some of these factors.

Absence of legal frameworks to ensure participation of farmers

After decades of public policy-making as the reserved domain of government, habits and mindsets are well established. Prior to the 1980s, smallholder farmers' organisations in Africa tended to be set up to achieve nation-building objectives, and were often considered as an operational arm of government's programmes (CTA, 2003). After the Economic Structural Adjustment Programmes of the 1990s, which led to the dismantling of public institutions, they inherited the responsibility to fulfil the value-chain functions previously performed by government agencies (for instance, input provision, credit, marketing, storage and extension), leaving policy-making as the sole focus of government (EC-DG Commission, 2007). Even if the policy space is now theoretically opening up, in practice government is still impregnated by previous long-standing types of relationships in the way it sees and relates to farmers' organisations today. On the farmers' side, lack of awareness, experience, resources and confidence prevent them from taking advantage of this new opportunity to get involved in the policy space.

Furthermore, in the absence of effective formal consultation spaces in the public-policy environment, it is difficult for smallholder farmers to assert their positions, as their lobbying capacities as marginalised members of the society are weak. Smallholder farmers' participation in policy-making processes can only be enabled by putting in place and enforcing legal frameworks that make multi-stakeholder participation mandatory in any policy processes, as benchmarks of success and acceptability of the outcome. These must include mandatory measures to be used and indicators to be deployed with regard to participation of non-state actors in policy processes.

Lack of time and resources devoted to consultation in policy processes

Even if multi-stakeholder consultation is recognised as a 'must' in policy processes, actual implementation can be hampered by lack of financial and human resources. Whereas most of sub-Saharan African states are poor in terms of available public finances and their institutions rather weak, conducting effective consultation can be protracted and demand substantial time and other resources. Particularly, consulting smallholder farmers can turn out to be a tedious and expensive exercise since, on one hand, they constitute a large and widespread population, and on the other, they might be little aware of, or educated on, policy matters.

In a globalised world where things seem to go ever faster every day, calendars of domestic policy processes might also be dictated by international agendas and schedules, which rarely take into account the constraints that are peculiar to African countries, including poor communication and transport infrastructures, weak technical capacities in terms of policy development, and poor financial resources. These constraints impose substantial time requirements for the least activity to be carried out. Effective multi-stakeholder consultations might be sacrificed upon the altar of the lack of time.

Lack of recognition of the importance of involving farmers in policy-making processes

Smallholder farmers might be difficult stakeholders to involve in policy process, mainly due to their weak capacities in policy development and their lack of effective organisation to speak with one voice. For policy-makers, it is easier to engage with agricultural experts or organisations that work with farmers, particularly NGOs. These have been showing a growing propensity to speak on behalf of farmers. Rashid Pertev noted that the absence of farmers' voices in most policy and programme dialogue forums has resulted in an escalation of various individuals, organisations and institutions claiming to speak for and on behalf of smallholder farmers (Pertney, n.d.). He pointed out that, in turn, the enthusiasm with which other people are ready to speak on behalf of farmers has often made the lack of the farmers' voices unnoticed. According to him, in most African countries, NGOs have now become an alternative voice of farmers. However, the legitimacy and representativeness of these organisations are questionable. They rarely put in place adequate mechanisms and structures for thorough consultations with smallholder farmers, which would yet be a minimum prerequisite before boasting about speaking for farmers. These organisations sometimes take advantage of the public dialogue platforms to first and foremost present their own opinions, perceptions and ideas, which might be different from those of smallholder farmers. Regrettably, failing to check the authenticity of these organisations, public authorities often wholly accept them as the voice of farmers, locking the space for a genuine representation of smallholder farmers. As a result, ownership of the process outcomes might be missed and their relevance defective (that is, not being demand driven).

Poor representative structures of smallholder farmers in the society

Pertev (n.d.) noted that to enable farmers to engage in a meaningful dialogue with the rest of society, they should have legitimate representative structures from the grassroots to the international level. When it comes to mobilising farmers into units that speak with one voice beyond the village, one cannot but notice that southern Africa lags behind compared to other regions in the continent.

In most SADC countries, there is only one national farmers' organisation (FO) which provides a forum for smallholder farmers to discuss their common wishes and aspirations and which champions their views as a bona-fide representative. Up until 2010, there was still no national independent structure that represented smallholder farmers in Lesotho and Swaziland. There is still none in the Democratic Republic of Congo, and in Angola, the UNACA (Confederação das Associações de Camponeses e Cooperativas Agro-Pecuárias de Angola), which supposedly represents farmers, is actually a parastatal agency as opposed to a purely farmer-based organisation.

The problem is compounded by the limited understanding and appreciation amongst ordinary smallholder farmers of the importance and basic concepts of FOs. Most of them are not conversant with the roles these organisations can play and how they (farmers) could benefit from participating and mobilising their own resources to defend their interests. On the other hand, FOs have failed to demonstrate tangible benefits accruing to their members. Additionally, achieving fair representation across a wide spectrum of interest is very challenging whilst FOs have to represent the interests of a diverse membership. Leaders tend to be commercially oriented, older males, with larger land holdings and members of the rural elite; yet the organisations have to ensure that the interests of all their members, including smaller farmers, women and young producers, are fairly represented and their needs adequately served.

Weak understanding of policy processes within the farmers' communities

Policy formulation and monitoring is a complex process, all the more so in a globalising world with more sophisticated national and international rules characterised by stringent and changing requirements. Effective participation requires not only an understanding of the issues, but also an understanding of the different stages of policy development and the actors involved at each and every stage. With high levels of illiteracy and limited access to education and information in most countries in the region, this understanding is a big challenge for smallholder farmers and their organisations. At most, they are only able to react to policies when consulted, which limits their impacts in terms of being influential.

Inadequate human and financial capacities of smallholders' organisations

Effective participation in policy processes requires technical capacities in a wide range of activities, including researching updated facts and evidence about the issue under consideration, consulting with relevant people and institutions, analysing existing policies, developing one's own sound policy positions, formulating parameters for negotiations, establishing networks and alliances, and finally, concretely engaging policy-makers. Moreover, in a globalised economy, policy formulation and monitoring have become more and more demanding, requiring highly specialised knowledge and extensive time. Performing these activities requires substantial funds. The protracted nature of most policy processes requires adequate staying power and also adds to the financial burden.

All these requirements are, for the most part, far beyond the capacities of small-holder farmers and their organisations, as they mostly rely on the fees from their members (who are few in number and have limited incomes) and little funding generally bound to project activities. There has also been a tendency amongst southern African smallholder farmers' organisations to underestimate the importance of investing in policy development and monitoring. Priority is always given to their core functions of production and marketing of agricultural products, the underlying argument being that 'one cannot eat policy'. Without facts and figures and sound analyses to back up their policy positions, the participation of smallholder farmers remains mere rhetoric, susceptible to being driven by emotions, which eventually often undermines their credibility in the policy process.

The poor image of smallholder farmers' organisations

Farmers have also failed to get adequate representation in policy processes due to the poor image and perception that policy-makers have of their organisations and representatives. Farmers in most southern African countries have not managed to build representative organisations that are legitimate, credible and accountable. As a result, policy-makers are reluctant to engage with them. Since farmers' leaders often fail to consolidate their power base, in the eyes of policy-makers they seem to represent their own interests and not those of farmers. A reputation based on trust, transparency and the capacity to cooperate with other organisations, as well as proper accountability to ensure that the outcomes of the policy intervention comply with the demands of member farmers are of paramount importance to policy-makers. Lastly, in some cases, smallholders' representative structures have failed to establish alliances with other organisations, when such alliances could help them strengthening their position and image.

Despite the structural challenges they face, African smallholder farmers need to reclaim their space in the policy arena and to take their rightful position in policy dialogue processes. It is promising that more and more institutions (both public and private) have now acknowledged this necessity to allow for sustainable development in the agricultural sector. This realisation, however, first has to materialise in the establishment of legitimate, accountable and capable representative organisations, which requires concrete commitment and support.

Role of professional farmers' organisations in enhancing smallholder farmers' participation in policy process

Farmers' organisations (FOs) can be defined as entities created to organise the relationships between the concerned group of farmers and the outside world, playing a 'bridging' function between farmers and other actors, such as input suppliers, financial institutions, produce retailers or processors and policy-makers (Mercoiret, 1999). A further categorisation differentiates FOs on the basis of their functions, such as commodity-based groups or general interest groups (Wennink *et al.*, 2008). Commodity-based groups are concerned mainly with organising farmers to produce and market a specific commodity, while general interest groups are concerned with defending and protecting the interests of all farmers through policy lobbying and advocacy. The latter are the most relevant to policy processes. They may operate at local, national, regional and continental levels.

Professional farmers' organisations have the potential to play a pivotal role in transforming the weak position of individual smallholder farmers in the society into strong legal entities that contribute positively to the social and economic advancement of the farming community, which eventually will have positive consequences in terms of poverty alleviation and economic growth on the continent.

Characteristics of a professional farmers' organisation

It is the prime role of an FO to consolidate the different views of many farmers into one united voice and to make it heard by bringing it to the policy arenas. Moreover, in terms of mandate and legitimacy, it must be the sole responsibility of FOs as the bona-fide voice of farmers to perform effective representation of farmers.

An important feature of any FO that is striving to be an efficient representative organisation is its ability to identify and consolidate its power base. The power of an organisation is derived from a combination of legitimacy and credibility, as well as financial capacity, and the three are closely linked. The legitimacy of an FO comes from the extension and composition of its membership, such as the gender ratio, age ratio, holding size and crop types. The more members an organisation has across the diversified spectrum of farmers, the more the power it will have to influence. Decision-makers always look for optimum public opinion; as such, any advocacy activity that has support from the majority is likely to receive attention and action from them. As this requires the mobilisation of a large and loyal base of supporters, a difficult challenge for national umbrella organisations participating in global discussions is that they must remain true to local members' interests, which may be widely varied. Maintaining open channels of communication with their memberships at the local, regional and national levels is imperative to overcome this challenge.

In summary, in terms of policy representation, a professional FO should, as a minimum, demonstrate the following:

- Representation: The organisation should have a significant number of members, with all segments represented, ideally in similar proportions to those present in the sector, including in the leadership (for instance, women, youth, per commodity). This is the case with an organisation such as the Zambian National Farmers' Union which has membership across the board and from various stakeholders within the agriculture sector. The variety of its membership and its wide coverage gives it the strength and clout to represent farmers.
- Functional structures: Organisational structures should be functional at all

levels, from grassroots to the highest level. Structures should operate according to good governance principles, with consultative internal decision-making processes, and application of the subsidiarity principle, especially for apex organisations. The National Smallholder Farmers' Association of Malawi (NASFAM) is a good example of an organisation that has functional structures from grassroots to the national level. The clubs at local level are connected to the national level through intermediary structures.

- Efficient communication channels: The organisation should have communication channels that enable extensive consultation internally and within coalitions/alliances, from the grassroots to the international level. These channels also need to reach out to policy-makers. At issue is to help farmers to understand the views of policy-makers and at the same time to enable policy-makers understand the views of farmers.

- Evidence-based policy intervention: The organisation should have strong evidence-based policy analysis and development capacities, including the ability to collect relevant qualitative and quantitative information to elaborate sound policy positions and proposals.

- Strong advocacy capacity: The organisation should be able to strategise its advocacy by identifying the objectives of the advocacy, possible alliances, targets, and most appropriate and cost-effective means to implement the strategy. Then it needs to be able to engage concretely in policy dialogue.

- Proactiveness: The organisation should analyse situations in advance and engage spontaneously in the policy dialogue instead of being reactive. It should also make farmers' voices heard through targeted campaigns.

- Accountability: The organisation should ensure transparent management and accountability to both members and partners.

- Autonomous: The organisation should be independent from any external influence such as government and donors/development agencies, and make decisions based on facts at its disposal and its own analysis. Moreover, it should also strive for ultimate financial autonomy while ensuring the diversification of financing sources.

These principles are important in allowing FOs to build credibility, from both farmers and policy-makers, but also from financial partners. In turn, a strong credibility will allow for the mobilisation of more smallholder farmers to become members, hence offering representation to a broader population and strengthening the FO's basis and legitimacy. Credibility is also essential to becoming an influential stakeholder and leveraging more finance to pursue the organisation's advocacy activities. The end-result of this iterative and exponential process is an increased influence of genuine smallholder farmers' views on agricultural matters, as well as enhanced ownership of policy outcomes, which are both essential to put in place and implement relevant and efficient policies aimed at fostering rural development and growth.

Best practices in southern Africa

There are best practices and promising experiences in southern Africa with regard to professional FOs that successfully represent smallholder farmers' positions in agricultural policy processes. The following two examples from Malawi and Zambia are some of the success stories where smallholder farmers have been able to influence policies.

In Malawi, the National Smallholder Farmers' Association of Malawi (NASFAM) is the largest independent, smallholder-owned membership organisation. It operates throughout Malawi with field-based operations and organisational structures from the grassroots level up to the national level. NASFAM recently conducted an advocacy campaign for changing a fiscal policy that was imposing a withholding tax from smallholder farmers' proceeds. This policy was seen by farmers as discriminatory. The campaign adopted varied approaches. They carried out an in-depth study of the issue, which was used to pressurise public authorities from different angles, including the parliamentary committee on agriculture, participation in key national policy formulation forums and various government in-stated task forces, dialogue engagement with the Malawi Revenue Authority and other relevant government departments. At the same time, NASFAM organised a policy platform and a national policy symposium to discuss the issue with its members and other stakeholders. It also participated extensively in radio panel discussions and radio presentations in which the contentious issue was discussed. As a result, NASFAM was able to achieve a total exemption from this tax on the smallholder farmers (SACAU, 2008). The success of the intervention by NASFAM could be attributed to several factors, including a well-recognised organisation that has a well-defined membership, a well-structured organisation that enables adequate consultation and support from the grassroots basis, the use of accurate facts to support the intervention, the identification of appropriate advocacy targets and the associated approach used, the setting of a clear policy agenda, and the effective use of relevant media houses.

In Zambia, since the legal and policy frameworks allowed FOs to transform from state-supported rural enterprises into independent farmer-run businesses, the Zambia National Farmers' Union (ZNFU) has grown into an exemplary national FO. With a broad-based membership drawn from smallholder farmers and large-scale farmers, but also including corporate members, commodity or specialised associations, the national agri-business chamber and associate members, the organisation is well structured, has substantial capacity and enjoys a good image, to the extent that it is recognised as a key partner by the government, is a key member in president's committees and has managed to influence policies in many instances. In 2009 for example, ZNFU succeeded in lobbying the Zambian government for a wheat importation ban to protect the local wheat industry against cheap imports, which would have resulted in weakening the economic situation of thousands of farmers as a result of non-profitable sales. Government responded positively and issued a statutory instrument banning the importation of wheat and wheat products into the country. As a result, local producers managed to sell around 40,000 mega-tons of unsold wheat[3] at acceptable price.

Through its specific engagement with the Ministry of Finance and National Planning on national budgets, ZNFU was also able to influence government to remove the Value Added Tax (VAT) on agricultural equipment for smallholder farmers, which constituted a significant financial burden to them. Recently, they have also lobbied for the formation of a committee to look specifically at ways to encourage financial institutions to continue to lend to agriculture. Such a committee is now established, headed by the secretary to the national treasury and with ZNFU as a member, it could have a major impact on supporting smallholder farming in Zambia (ZNFU, 2009). ZNFU has been able to achieve these results thanks to among other things, their capacity to demonstrate effectively their importance to the authority; the recognition by the authority that they are a mouthpiece of farmers; the wide representativeness of their structure, which gives them political clout; and their ability to gather relevant data and provide sound analysis for their lobbying activities.

At regional level, the Southern Africa Confederation of Agricultural Unions (SACAU) was formed to give a voice to southern African farmers in a context of regional integration and globalisation. Its membership is opened to national farmers' unions and regional commodity associations. The prime mandate of SACAU is to engage with policy-makers at regional, continental and global levels to defend the interest of the agricultural sector in the region. SACAU is already recognised by many stakeholders in the policy-making processes as a main dialogue partner, including the Regional Economic Communities, African Union (AU) and NEPAD, as well as research and development agencies. It actively participates in all policy processes that deal with agriculture in the region, directly or indirectly (particularly trade), notably by sitting on technical committees, commenting on draft documents, and attending public meetings. These include the Comprehensive African Agriculture Development Process (CAADP), the Southern Africa Development Community Regional Agriculture Policy (SADC-RAP), the Common Market for Eastern and Southern Africa (COMESA) strategic plan for agriculture, the COMESA Alliance for Commodity Trade in Eastern and Southern Africa (ACTESA) programme, the World Trade Organisation (WTO) standards-setting processes, the African Union (AU) land policy framework and the World Development Report of 2008. SACAU has also initiated a policy development programme aimed at elaborating evidence-based positions on agricultural issues that are of concern to southern African farmers, as expressed through SACAU's Annual General Meeting. To date, it has issued three position papers on Aid for Trade, Food Aid and Climate Change, and both the background discussion papers and positions are widely disseminated to farmers, via SACAU members and other stakeholders. In terms of alliance, SACAU is

---

3   http://www.znfu.org.zm/index.php?option=com_content&view=article. Accessed December 2009.

a co-founding member of the Pan-African Farmers Platform that was created in May 2008 by the four regional farmers' networks of sub-Saharan Africa. The platform aims at joining forces to promote the resurgence of African agriculture so that the sector can fulfil its essential functions. SACAU is also very active in promoting effective representative structures and approaches amongst its members. Furthermore, the emergence of this regional structure has facilitated the mobilisation of financial resources from bilateral and multilateral aid agencies for national FOs in the region, allowing the improvement of their organisational capacities and their technical resources.

Conclusion

The importance of smallholder farmers' participation in agriculture-related policy processes cannot be overemphasised in the objective of achieving successful agricultural outcomes in sub-Saharan Africa. The evidence of a willingness on the part of governments and other stakeholders to involve them in policy formulation and monitoring can be observed, which is promising. However, African smallholder farmers are yet to take advantage of the opportunities that are availed to them to participate, mainly due to weak representative structures.

As a means of pursuing farmers' economic, social and political objectives, professional FOs could potentially be a significant force in driving agricultural and rural development on the continent. They must be recognised as the legitimate voices of smallholder farmers, and it is critical to promote them and support and strengthening their capacities if full participation of farmers in agri-policy processes is to be realised. However, realising their potential will take not only an enormous effort on their part, in terms of commitment to organisational development and proactive policy engagement. It will also need a determined drive by donors and international agencies to help them to meet the many challenges they are still facing, including those to do with representativeness, governance, skills, and communication, without compromising their effective empowerment. A strong and proactive legal and political commitment from African governments will also be required to redress a situation in which the majority has been kept voiceless for decades.

At stake here is the unlocking of the enormous potential of sub-Saharan agriculture in terms of food security, economic growth and social justice, not only for the continent but for the entire planet in a context of population growth and climate change.

References

CTA (2003). *Meeting the Needs of Farmers' Organisations in a Changing World*. Annual Report. Brussels, Belgium: 36.

EC-DG Commission (2007). Advancing African agriculture: Proposal for continental and regional level cooperation on agricultural development in Africa. Discussion paper from the EC-DG Commission, Brussels, Belgium (January).

Food and Agriculture Organisation (FAO) (2009). The special challenge for sub-Saharan Africa. Issues brief for the High-Level Expert Forum on How to Feed the World in 2050, Rome: 4 (12–13 October).

Mercoiret, M.R. (1999). Contribution to the workshop on Producer Organisations Empowerment. Workshop proceedings. Washington.

Pertev, R. (n.d.). The Role of Farmers and Farmers' Organizations. Mediterranean Committee of the International Federation of Agricultural Producers (IFAP), Paris, France.

SACAU-DFID/Commark Trust. (2008). Regional Standards Programme Project Reports, 2007–2008. Centurion, South Africa.

SACAU (2008). Aid for Trade and southern African farmers: Key issues and possible policy positions. Discussion Paper No. 1. Centurion, South Africa (December).

SACAU (2008). Lobby Guide for Farmers' Organisations; 54–5.

Syngeta Foundation (2009). *Smallholder Mapping and Characteristics: Understanding Smallholder Farmers.* http://www.syngentafoundation.org/index.cfm?pageID=297. Accessed: 31 October 2009.

Wennink, B., Heemskerk, W., & Nederlof, S. (2008). Strengthening the role of farmers' organisations in agricultural innovations systems: Case studies from Benin, Rwanda and Tanzania. Paper presentation at Innovation Africa Symposium, Kampala, Uganda (20–23 November).

ZNFU (2009). Zambia National Farmers' Union, 104th Congress Report: 14–15.

Conclusion

Leslie Nyagah

Main lessons

Smallholder agriculture contributes most of the income, jobs and food production in Africa. Despite their identified role in African society livelihood initiatives, smallholder farmers still face several challenges, which include limited finance and limited access to credit and capital for investments required to accelerate agricultural growth. Recently, governments and donors alike have begun to use different instruments to promote the required growth in smallholder agriculture. Among the most popular support tools is government spending, which is a direct and efficient method, but its use remains low and tardy in most African countries due to poor policy environments and inefficient public expenditure and service delivery processes. While public spending on agriculture would most likely result in reduced poverty and increased production, there are great differences in expenditure patterns. For instance, in a country such as Malawi, government expenditure on the farm input subsidy programme has produced the highest return on agricultural investment, but this has not translated into the same outcome in Tanzania. However, by examining the composition of total expenditure across countries one is able to piece together a pattern that reflects the priorities of government intervention in agricultural support and reveals more variances than commonalities.

Most African states have failed to meet their commitment of increasing national budgets for agriculture to 10 per cent as per the Maputo Declaration of 2003. A southern African country such as Malawi, however, has been able to increase its budget allocation to agriculture to more than 10 per cent of its national budget. While most national budgets, as in the case of Malawi and Tanzania, are split between recurrent and development components, it is important to establish how much of the expenditure is actually going towards smallholder farmers' needs and welfare. Most government and donor resources tend to be focused on the recurrent segment of the budget that supports overall administration or implementation in terms of service delivery to beneficiaries, while the development segment, which supports investment in long-term assets such as irrigation infrastructure and building of rural feeder roads, tends to be sidelined. A meaningful agricultural growth strategy aimed at supporting smallholder farmers' needs has to take shape and be aligned with recent promises of expenditure support. This may include financial support for public investments and policies, including crop and animal science, improved extension systems, and market-facilitating investments such as physical and communications infrastructure. It is common knowledge that African governments do not lack the overall public resources, but it is their political inability to transcend their inertia and radically transform the sector that is preventing growth.

With Africa's over-reliance on donor support for agricultural development, the recent worldwide economic crisis has meant less donor funds for smallholder farming projects, and they are finding it difficult to produce more with less financial resources. This is further complicated by an incessant disregard for property rights, tenure laws and declining natural resources, including water for agriculture. Increased public investment in rural areas and enterprises is difficult, if not unlikely, because of the nature of the urban capitalist society. There must be a new impetus for the efficient use of public investment resources within countries. This requires improved targeting and prioritisation of investments to achieve growth and poverty-alleviation goals, as well as improved efficiency within the agencies that provide public goods and services. Reliable information on the marginal effects of various types of government spending is crucial if sound investment choices are to be made by public and private enterprises. Despite the vast differences in South Africa's, Tanzania's and Malawi's modes of production, natural resources, socioeconomic conditions and size, the different investment choices that each country has made offer some important lessons for future public expenditure decisions.

Agricultural policies generally tend to be rhetorically pro-poor in approach, but have provided weak economic incentives to smallholder farmers in the rural areas. The stated objectives of many policies, strategies, programmes and projects in southern Africa favour smallholder farmers and the improved livelihood and nutritional conditions in the rural areas. Despite these promising objectives, the productivity of smallholder agriculture has continued to decline because of failures in the prioritisation and implementation of public expenditure support structures and the constant lack of participation of smallholder famers in local and regional policy planning and intervention committees. For example, while it has been noted that the fertiliser subsidy programme in Tanzania has increased over time, constraints in the distribution system, in terms of quality and reliability of supply chain vendors, have hamstrung the programme, to the detriment of smallholder farmers.

Despite the fact that smallholder farmers account for the majority of the farming population in most southern African countries, the logic of including them in decision-making and policy processes that affect their daily lives has not materialised. Most of the agricultural strategies, programmes and projects are hardly based on the needs of smallholder farmers, but are based on government capacity to deliver and available financial and human resources. Communication channels and access to information to enable smallholder farmers to participate in policy formulation and monitoring are still inadequate. Continental groups and regional economic blocs such as the African Union and Southern African Development Community (SADC) have become important sites for making decisions and commitments relating to the improvement of agriculture. However, a lack of effective organisation and representation of farmers at the local, national and regional level, has meant that their participation has generally been disjointed and muzzled.

In addition, the agricultural policy-making arena at local, national and regional levels has been occupied by aspiring political figures who do not articulate the true needs of the farmers – they treat the farmers as a passive electorate rather than active citizens who have a right to engaging in policy-making processes. The struggle that most smallholder farmers face (together with many other African citizens) is a failure to identify individuals and channels that can ultimately lead to change within their societies. As a result it is difficult to ascertain whether farmer organisations and their pressure groups have been able to influence agricultural policy and budget reform. For example, the apartheid state was highly interventionist in agricultural activities by means of their dominance over capital and market processes. This was enabled by a highly organised and racially exclusive farming hierarchy of small, medium and large farms. For the democratic government, which wants to entice black farmers and fund developmental projects, the issue will be how best to use sizable budget allocations, while at the same time addressing the governance aspects of agriculture. Do the South African governance structures allow for citizen participation in the identification and delivery of smallholder agricultural priorities and needs, and how will the government respond? Allocating more money to an agricultural sector that is still hierarchical in nature will not translate into changing attitudes and practices; however, an inclusive societal process to build citizen interest and capacity to develop and implement solutions does take time.

Manifesto for the future of public investment and governance in sub-Saharan Africa

More recently, smallholder agriculture in Africa has gained reasonable ground in revitalising the sector. However, common setbacks and push-back factors, such as the recent financial crisis and the ecological damage in most of Africa, will likely have an impact on food production and food security responses, albeit not immediately noticeable. Changes in donor and government attitudes have meant that there is a firm commitment to put the agricultural development agenda firmly back on the map, whilst concomitantly increasing financial and technical support to this sector. This shift in thinking has come about through a process of flash-point periods in history, when food insecurity has had a great impact on the global, political-economic architecture. For example, in the early 1990s African governments introduced the Structural Adjustment Programmes (SAPs). These programmes were intended to increase the performance of government departments, liberalise economies and introduce market economics, while dismantling farmer cooperatives and cutting public spending on social services such as education, social security and health. However, the outcome of these programmes was that there was a decline in agricultural performance, which decreased prices of agricultural produce, increased prices of agricultural inputs and disrupted local procurement procedures – these lingering effects of SAPs are, to some degree or another, still issues today.

The droughts of the early 1990s saw an intense period in which most African countries were aid-dependent, importing yellow maize to feed their starving citizens. The iconic image that captured the dire situation of the time was of a malnourished Ethiopian child sitting next to an American food aid parcel. The result of this catastrophe was that African countries who had cut their expenditure on agriculture in favour of social spending, and who had suffered cutbacks in donor financing to sectors such as agriculture, had to adopt a transformative agenda that focused more on food sovereignty and the nuances of how and by whom food is produced. The recent food riots that happened globally also gave credence to finding innovative ways to use public expenditure to enable food production. In Malawi, for example, the clarion call is for all Malawians to prioritise local agriculture in order to feed the local population. This has been achieved partly by mainstreaming public expenditure to agricultural support services, such as input and fertiliser subsidy programmes, and partly by recognising the multifunctional nature of agriculture which involves rural development and poverty reduction strategies.

In most African countries the commitments made to improving the agricultural sector have not materialised or translated into practical solutions. An example of this is the failure of most countries to adhere to the Maputo Declaration of allocating 10 per cent of the national budget to agriculture. Malawi is the only country within the southern Africa region to consistently meet the 10 per cent allocation to agriculture. Most others in the region have allocated between 5 and 10 per cent. Governments and donors alike have to view agriculture as a key strategic driver of national economies. They will have to increase their financial commitments to the sector in general terms, while aligning support to practical policy, growth and investment options that involve smallholder farmers in the broader economic growth strategies, while reducing rural poverty. In addition, countries will have to take cognisance of allocation efficiency and the quality of investments to the sector in order to ensure that allocated funds address development priorities effectively and target areas with the highest needs and returns.

Sustained agricultural growth cannot be attained by market share growth and increased investments alone. Governments, especially those in southern Africa, will have a key role to play in scaling up and radically transforming the smallholder agricultural environment. This may involve creating an environment conducive for agriculture in general and specifically aligning smallholder agricultural priorities with the Comprehensive African Agriculture Development Programme (CAADP) framework. The benefit of this is that it would ease implementation of policy and regulatory improvements to the sector, while providing support structures and compliance to agreed regional standards and norms such as infrastructural development, environmental protection and security over property.

Southern African governments will have to go through a rigorous process of priority setting for smallholder farmers' needs and find innovative ways to mainstream them into participatory policy-making processes. Involving national policy-making bodies such as parliaments in the participatory strategy formulation process may help to reduce the disconnection between participation and implementation. While participation is vital for smallholder agriculture, the process of implementation may include technical aspects which might reduce the participation of smallholder farmers who may not be technically inclined. Participatory agencies need to recognise how the promotion of participatory processes in sector governance can strengthen performance and outcomes rather than undermine institutions of democracy. Non-governmental organisations (NGOs) could also play a role in redefining and cementing citizen attitudes towards public policy change. This includes shifting priorities and resources while seeking new ways to promote local ownership of sector policies, and fostering adequate governance conditions for change, including transparent budget processes and inclusive citizenship in policy-making.

Most recent agricultural reform strategies have been focused on governance reform within the sector. The ongoing processes of democratisation, and civil participation in the way in which public functions are carried out and public resources are managed, safeguards against insidious corrupt practices in sectoral policymaking and generally improves agricultural performance. A vibrant and dynamic agricultural sector has been known to increase the incentives for the entry of new non-State actors in the agricultural value chain, and their involvement in processes such as food manufacturing, storage and retailing has increased due to a deregulated agricultural environment. However, in most southern African countries, the involvement of non-state actors has not necessarily mainstreamed smallholder farmers' initiatives to increase productivity. Their individualistic engagement in farming processes within the national framework may be construed as policyneutral and has generally supported the status quo. They have been lacklustre in expressing views on how the sector has to change according to social, agro-ecological, cultural contexts and policy confines, or nudging public actors towards a radical transformation of the sector.

The role of the State is to increase citizen participation in policy-making and to support sectoral growth through public policy and resources. However, increasing smallholder participation in agriculture policy-making and sector reforms remains a challenge, even in democratic arenas. Building responsive institutions that recognise and meet the needs of ordinary people through inclusive consultative processes, forming purposeful partnerships, creating legislative environments for participatory socioeconomic policy-making and promoting dialogue between relevant stakeholders aimed at reaching consensus may be some of the ways to overcome the governance dilemma at regional and national levels. The overarching aim is to create an informed citizenry who can define their own economic and political environments without turning themselves into passive recipients of regional and national policy. Whether this is achieved through popular democratic forms or neoliberal approaches, the end goal is to create an egalitarian society, participatory policy-making on issues of public welfare and for citizens to identify with issues that relate to social justice, basic rights and participation.

There is no 'one size fits all' solution to the plight of smallholder farmers in their national contexts. However, there is a need for a new paradigm shift that gives equal weight to the role of private actors, communities and civil society, local government and regional organisations to improve the livelihoods of smallholder farmers. This process may include a bold move towards building a broad consensus amongst actors on issues such as comparative advantages and the delegation of function in terms of co-production of activities that relate to smallholder agriculture. Most African governments have tended to follow a quick-fix approach to planning and implementation for the agricultural sector, translating social gains into political expediency. This often results in poor-quality service and delivery and financial unsustainability of government-provided agricultural support services. For radical interventions in smallholder agriculture to be successful, women and the youth have to be included. Increasing their capacity to improve agricultural production techniques and best practices should be strengthened to facilitate agricultural strategy beyond the farm gate to institutions that foster inclusivity in agricultural growth. How such an integrated pathway is fostered in a particular country should depend on past history, cultural contexts, what currently exists and what can be built on, as these factors can present serious obstacles later to the furtherance of women's rights, their inclusion in agricultural production and their ability to access economic assets and incentives.

Conclusion and policy implications

Public investment in smallholder agriculture

There is a need to understand that poverty and food insecurity generally correlate with geographical regions. If genuine investment in agriculture is to take place on the continent, it should start in countries and geographic agricultural zones in which poverty is prevalent. Investment should also specifically address smallholder farmers' priorities and should bolster existing socioeconomic outcomes and protection systems (whether it is on a national or local level). This could include priorities such as technology, infrastructure, roads, schools and clinics. Rather than treating these as stand-alone investments, they should be aligned to agricultural priorities, in particular those that are essential for smallholder farming to attain the overall national imperatives.

Complex geopolitical problems such as climate change and a downturn in large donor financing means that large-scale investments in raising the agricultural profile and output in Africa are unlikely, at least from a donor financing perspective. This places tremendous fiscal and political pressure on African governments to pursue agricultural development plans on their own, even when the majority of farmers are poor and in need of assistance. This means that governments have to understand agriculture in general in the context of multi-sectoral and equilibrium frameworks and not through a sectoral lens alone. A 'business un-usual' approach to smallholder agriculture needs to take place to address the issues of productivity and market orientation in tandem with issues of social protection and sustainability.

Improving the business climate in agriculture would provide leverage to access private sector capital for activities upstream and downstream from the farm. Removing regional barriers to agricultural trade, improving ancillary services such as reliable, renewable energy, providing soft loans and eliminating export taxation on agriculture would be significant in providing triggers for investment regimes and making domestic and regional agriculture more competitive.

Public and private expenditure can also be used to facilitate rural livelihood diversification schemes. Policy-makers have to be aware of what is being observed in the rural areas in order to be able to adapt policies to development and address cash constraints where appropriate. Livelihood diversification and non-farm employment has propelled smallholder households in a positive direction through the use of cash income and assets as collateral for farm investment and also by mitigating against the unpredictable nature of farming. Thus non-farm activities, such as the sale of traditional medicines and firewood, do complement the development patterns of smallholder agriculture in southern Africa.

Enhancing constructive participation of smallholder farmers in agro-food value chains

Farmer organisations are concentrated mainly in major towns and municipalities, and they find it increasingly difficult to operate in rural and remote locations. While farmer organisations have been significant stakeholders in smallholder agriculture policy-making and advocating for farmer rights, their inability to tap effectively into the rural masses, who sometimes view such organisations with scepticism and suspicion, has resulted in their inability to generate the legitimacy and ownership required to make and implement credible policies for smallholder agriculture at national and regional levels. This can be improved if farmer organisations are transformed into organisations that have far reaching influences due to their links and affiliations with the private sector, religious organisations, government departments and community-based organisations (CBOs) in order to deliver direct empowerment to rural communities through service delivery.

Gains in smallholder agriculture tend to be more effective in democratic societies that provide an environment conducive to engagement. Non-State actors and relevant stakeholders should encourage and participate in social movements that place good governance and the democratic agenda for food and farmer rights at the centre of the poverty eradication and development agenda. This will eventually produce momentum for citizen agency that will enable governments to listen to the demands for increased smallholder food production and to advance broad-based food systems that will eventually create an equitable food consumption base.

Farmers' organisations and civil society should be able to examine the policy and budget-making processes associated with smallholder agriculture and their associated outcomes. This way they are able to produce rigorous policy-relevant intervention plans to enable them to mobilise local, national and regional advocacy alliances. To do this, farmer organisations and civil society have to invest in human resource and skills capacity for policy and budget analysis and advocacy efforts.

The independent management and action approach adopted by farmer organisations, CSOs, NGOs, donors and governments has meant that policy approaches towards smallholder agriculture have failed to garner the necessary consensus and common voice required to reach a common meaningful solution. The way in which State and non-State actors relate to each other has to be shifted in order to increase public consciousness on the plight of smallholder farmers, and to spur constructive, open and stimulating public dialogue to call upon stronger donor, civil society and government engagement on smallholder intervention strategies.

References

Binswanger-Mkhize, H.P. & Pingali, P.L. (1988). *Technological Priorities for Farming in Sub-Saharan Africa*. The World Bank Research Observer Vol. 3, No. 1.

Binswanger-Mkhize, H.P. (2009). Challenges and opportunities for African agriculture and food security: High food prices, climate change, population growth, and HIV and Aids. Paper presented at expert meeting on How to Feed the World in 2050. Food and Agriculture Organization of the United Nations.

Chilonda, P., Olubode-Awosola, F., Minde, I., Njiwa, D. & Govereh, J. (2009). Monitoring of public spending in agriculture in southern Africa. Paper presented at the International Association of Agricultural Economists Conference, Beijing, China (16–22 August).

Cook, J. (2009). *Smallholder Agriculture and the Environment in a Changing Global Context*. World Wide Fund for Nature (WWF) Macroeconomics Program Office, Washington, DC, USA.

Fan, S., Brzeska, J. & Shields, G. (2007). *Investment Priorities for Economic Growth and Poverty Reduction: 2020 Focus Brief on the World's Poor and Hungry People*. Washington, DC: International Food Policy Research Institute.

Fan, S., Omilola, B. & Lambert, M. (2009). *Public Spending for Agriculture in Africa: Trends and Composition*. ReSAKSS Working Paper No. 28.

Haggblade, S. (2007). *Returns to Investment in Agriculture*. Lusaka: Zambia Food Security Research Project.

Jayne, T.S., Mather, D. & Mghenyi, E. (2006). *Smallholder Farming Under Increasingly Difficult Circumstances: Policy and Public Investment Priorities for Africa*. Washington, DC: The United States Agency for International Development.

Jayne, T.S., Mason, N., Myers, R., Ferris, J., Mather, D. & Beaver, M. (2010). *Patterns and Trends in Food Staples Markets in Eastern and Southern Africa: Toward the Identification of Priority Investments and Strategies for Developing Markets and Promoting Smallholder Productivity Growth*. MSU International Development Working Paper No. 104.

Matshe, I. (2009). Boosting smallholder production for food security: Some approaches and evidence from studies in sub-Saharan Africa. *Agrekon*, Vol. 48, No. 4.

Pingali, P.L., Bigot, Y. & Binswanger, H. (1987). *Agricultural Mechanization and the Evolution of farming Systems in Sub-Saharan Africa*. Baltimore, Maryland: Johns Hopkins University Press.

Pingali, P. (2003). Sustaining food security in developing world: The top five policy challenges. *Quarterly Journal of International Agriculture*, Vol. 42, No. 3: 261–272.

Resnick, D. & Birner, R. (2008). *Agricultural Strategy Development in West Africa: The False Promise of Participation?* Washington, DC: International Food Policy Research Institute.

Salami, A., Kamara, A.B. & Brixiova, Z. (2010). *Smallholder Agriculture in East Africa: Trends, Constraints and Opportunities*. African Development Bank

Scherr, S.J., Wallace, C. & Buck, L. (2010). Agricultural innovation for food security and poverty reduction in the 21st century: Issues for Africa and the world. Issues paper for *State of the World 2011: Innovations that Nourish the Planet*. Published by Eco-agriculture Partners 2010, Washington DC.

Southern Africa Trust (2008). *Who will feed the Poor? The Future of Food Security for Southern Africa*. A policy discussion paper printed by the Southern Africa Trust (SAT), Midrand, South Africa.

Timmer, P. (2005). *Agriculture and Pro-poor Growth: An Asian Perspective*. Centre for Global Development Working Paper No. 63.

Keynote speech on governance and small-scale agriculture in southern Africa

ARCHBISHOP NJONGONKULU NDUNGANE

Distinguished Ladies and Gentlemen, I am honoured to be part of this conference on Governance and Small-scale Agriculture.

This conference could not have come at a better time than this when there is a strong realisation that targeting small-scale famers is one of the key strategies to ending hunger. I am delighted that the rest of the continent continues to take the African small-scale agricultural revolution priorities to heart, although their significance in advancing the continents' development imperatives is only being realised now.

Ladies and gentlemen, God has blessed Africa with land, rivers, lakes, technology, and the good will of our people in order to meet our needs and not our greed. Through our liberation struggles for land in Africa, it cost us blood, sweat and tears to gain our freedom. Therefore, in our watch and time, we cannot afford to let our children go hungry. It is immoral to have so many hungry people in the midst of plenty resources. What is required of us now is to flex our muscles and stiffen our spines to end hunger now without fail!

Dear friends, as you are already aware, poverty continues to be one of the biggest challenges in Africa, with between 250 and 300 million Africans suffering from extreme poverty and hunger. And with the advent of the financial global crisis, it is estimated that 100 million more people will fall deeper into poverty.

Actually, let me spare you the gloomy picture about the poverty situation in Africa; you already know this and you have heard this over and over again. The tragedy in Africa is that we have talked so much about hunger and poverty that it has lost its significance. It is a calamity that it would seem that the idea of malnourished children and of people dying of hunger does not scare us anymore!

The urge to fight and end poverty is rapidly fading away and the sense of urgency completely lost among many key role players. The dream to meet the MDGs by 2015 remains a pipe dream for many, especially those in Africa. If halving the population living in poverty and ending hunger by 2015, as enshrined in the MDGs, is such an important goal for our governments and for all of us, it makes sense that food security and agricultural development become our top priorities. Small-scale agriculture, specifically focused on women, becomes one of the key escape routes, if not the sure way, of preventing people from dying of hunger and poverty. Three simple things come to mind on what needs to happen for African agriculture to emerge out of the current woods and boom.

Firstly, commitments already made have to be operationalised

Since the 1980s, agriculture in Africa has suffered policy reversals and resource deficiencies. But since Maputo Protocol in 2003, a number of political commitments have been made in respect of increased national resources allocated to agriculture. Under the Comprehensive African Agricultural Development Programme (CAADP) donors have pledged to reverse the decline of Official Development Assistance (ODA) to agriculture. In September 2009, the G8 leaders reiterated the need to coordinate funding when they pledged US$ 20 billion to help developing countries out of the food security crisis and to support long-term agricultural development. However, in reality money has often not been put where the committers' mouths are. Civil society organisations need to hold their governments accountable to ensure that these commitments translate into tangible results to benefit the poor farmers. Seven years into the Maputo protocol, which pledged to allocate 10 per cent of national budgets to agriculture, the sector remains undernourished or outrightly starved.

Isn't it ironic that the sector that feeds both the rich and the poor alike should be receiving on average 5 per cent of the national budgets and that only five countries should be walking the Maputo talk?

Isn't it sad that there are still more than 17 countries in Africa that spend less than 5 per cent of their budgets on agriculture?

Unfortunately, that is the current status quo.

Secondly, the resources so committed have to be correctly directed

Resources have to be directed to farm families, especially women, to enable them to access improved technologies such as improved seeds, organic and inorganic fertilisers, and irrigation to complement rain-fed farming. I think African governments have a responsibility to boost agricultural investment, foster the uptake of new technology, develop infrastructure (for example, roads, warehouses and wholesale facilities), and improve access to credit, particularly for small-scale and medium-scale farmers. Post-harvest produce management and access to markets also deserve attention. Specifically, governments need to take measures that favour access for small-scale farmers to improved inputs, that support agricultural research and development, and that spread knowledge about effective farming and farm management, and access to markets (both local and international ones). An example from China shows us how in just two decades, China has made a remarkable leap from being a small apple producer to becoming the world's largest apple producer and exporter. In the early 1980s, China produced less than three million tons of apples per year. By 2007, more than 42 per cent of all apples produced in the world originated in China (FAO, 2008). This can be attributed to governance mechanisms which were formed that linked small-scale apple farmers in China with export markets. These institutional innovations have improved the efficiency of price transmission and generated higher profit margins for various actors in the supply chain, in particular for small-scale farmers. And to mitigate the possible negative impacts of modern market development on small farmers, several recent surveys showed that farmer cooperatives, which increased farm contact, were all ways of improving small farmers' market involvement and bargaining powers. Such models can be replicated in some parts of Africa.

In another practical example, a civil society organisation in Ghana, called Esoko, has devised a mobile phone system that empowers local small-scale famers to have access to information about the markets, pricing, weather etc. Small-scale famers in Africa are normally taken advantage of by traders who travel to farm gates to buy their harvest, with no up-to-date information from beyond their villages or neighbouring villages, no resources to acquire that information and rarely do these famers have the bargaining power necessary to increase their revenues. Hence, the increased mobile coverage and access in these remotes villages has empowered the small-scale farmers to be in control of their harvests.

Thirdly, there is a need to ensure that there is sustainability of food security and agriculture initiatives

This would require that small-scale farmers tap into centres of excellence and research institutions in order to draw on their skills and knowledge (for example, how to conserve water and use and transfer new technology). Strategies to avoid disasters and negative effects of climate change should be adopted. So where does governance apply in all of this?

My answer is a simple one: if and when a government successfully feeds its nation, it should be regarded as one of the key indicators for good governance. African countries must stop looking to others and get on with the job of guaranteeing food security for their own people. Countries such as Malawi, Burkina Faso, Mali, Ethiopia and Senegal are demonstrating that it can be done. A few others, like Mozambique, Egypt and Tanzania, are inching the way towards the 10 per cent target. The rest, particularly the 17 which spend less than 5 per cent, must pull up their socks. There is enough good practice by peers for them to emulate! But words, words and words will not feed the poor! We need action, implementation and political muscle and will to feed the hungry. Putting policies on paper, committing and planning to act are not enough. There is a need to implement policies and strategies to end hunger. The right to food is enshrined in the Universal Declaration of Human Rights. It is an inalienable one. There is no excuse for people to go hungry amidst abundant natural and human resources. Two weeks ago, during the Southern Africa Trust and *Mail & Guardian*'s Drivers of Change Awards, I was privileged to sit next to the President of Malawi, HE Bingu wa Mutharika. He said that he will go out with a begging bowl to feed his people. He has told the international community, who refused to provide subsidies for his farmers, to keep their money! He has managed, using the right leadership and political will to turn Malawi from being a food-deficit to a food-surplus economy.

Ladies and gentlemen, I wish his peers would emulate the steps that he has taken to ensure that the country moves from a food deficit to a food surplus. For me, that is a good indicator of good governance.

Before I end, ladies and gentlemen, I think it is of utmost importance for me to touch on the subject of partnership in this issue of accelerating small-scale agriculture.

Within the development agenda currently, there is a deep realisation that effective partnership is the only way that we will achieve any significant progress. Africans, even those in the diaspora, are looking for effective partnerships within the continent through regional integration. More and more, civil society should be seeking for ways of engaging constructively with decision-makers with the understanding that we all want the same things.

We need to strengthen any mechanisms that we can to enhance talking to each other openly, appreciating one another's roles, expertise and constraints to achieve our common objectives

Lastly, it is my great hope that the conference will yield the much needed ideas, partnerships and strategies to ensure that we end hunger now

I thank you!

Archbishop Njongonkulu Ndungane
African Monitor

Keynote speech on governance and small-scale agriculture in southern Africa

DR JOE PHAAHLA

The Right Reverend, Archbishop Njongonkulu Ndungane,
The Executive Director of Idasa, Mr Paul Graham,
Ms Ruth Hall from the Institute for Poverty, Land and Agrarian Studies,
Ladies and Gentlemen.

On the 16 October 2009 we celebrated World Food Day in a village called Muyexe in Limpopo. The occasion was attended by several ministers of government, Members of Parliament, members of executive councils responsible for agriculture, traditional leaders, FAO country representatives and several other key stakeholders, as well as the members of the communities themselves.

The irony might not have been lost to some, that we chose to celebrate this day at this desolate village where most people never know where their next meal is going to come from; a village where unemployment is almost a way of life. This is a village whose inhabitants hardly have any place of abode to speak of, unless, for instance, one regards a dilapidated mud house as a home.

Ladies and gentlemen, the main reason for the choice of venue for this celebration was to highlight the miserable plight of some of our rural populace. It is the same reason that saw a number of government ministers, MECs and others coming to the village for the occasion so that they could see for themselves how the other half lives, so that as government, our response to their needs should be coordinated, integrated, multi-dimensional and sustainable.

Food insecurity, defined as a lack of access to adequate, safe and nutritious food, is closely associated with poverty. It can ultimately only be addressed as part of a broader attack on poverty, which includes direct employment and income.

While there may be adequate food at national level, a great percentage of the population has insufficient food or is exposed to an imbalanced diet. That is why government is placing emphasis on food security at household level and this can only be achieved if small-scale farmers are encouraged and supported.

I believe that increasing productivity in small-scale agriculture will lead to significant broader economic growth. The rate and extent of development in a more diversified farming sector – especially in small-scale agriculture – will determine such growth.

Small-scale farming is a feature of the South African landscape. That is why, since 1994, the South African government has spent billions of rands supporting this segment of the farming sector. I know this statement may raise a few eyebrows, but let us for a moment take a 6,000-strong community that has claimed back 6,000 hectares.

In essence, each household owns and farms on one hectare, which to me translates into a small-scale enterprise. The only difference is that the community works like a cooperative.

Through the Proactive Land Acquisition Strategy, the department has spent millions of rands buying agricultural land, which individuals have leased from government with a view to buy, as and when they have accumulated enough capital. The land varies in size from 500 to 1,000 hectares. This is also hardly large scale.

There is considerable international evidence of the efficiency and labour-intensity of small-farm agriculture in a wide variety of agro-ecological circumstances, although this may not necessarily apply in all parts of this country. Furthermore, small-scale farmers tend to make crop choices different from those made by large farmers. Most importantly, they tend to allocate more of their land to staple foods, vegetables and drought-resistant crops that are less risky and also more labour-intensive than the mono-crop agriculture preferred on large farms.

Small-scale farmers also tend to use their land more productively for larger parts of the year than large-scale farmers. In particular, small-scale farmers' access to family labour often encourages them to make year-round use of available irrigation water. Their production is indirectly labour-creating as well because it results in income flows to low-income rural dwellers that tend to purchase services, building materials and consumer goods from local small-scale rural services and industries.

This is all the more reason why the Department of Rural Development has been mandated to ensure that the concept of the Comprehensive Rural Development Programme (CRDP) succeeds. For us to realise success in this regard, we are currently reviewing some of our land reform products such as Land Redistribution for Agricultural Development so that recipients of such products engage in sustainable enterprises.

For the Comprehensive Rural Development Programme to succeed there needs to be agrarian transformation for a better future. Agrarian transformation means a rapid and fundamental change in the power relations between natural resources, livestock and crop farming and the community.

The Land Care Programme of the Department of Agriculture, Fisheries and Forestry plays an indispensable role in the management of this power relation. Government will facilitate the establishment of rural agro-industries, cooperatives, cultural initiatives, other business initiatives, leading to vibrant local markets. This is our vision for vibrant, equitable and sustainable rural communities. This, ladies and gentlemen, thus means and calls for greater inter-sectoral cooperation with government departments (for example, the Departments of Agriculture, Trade and Industry and Arts and Culture) and the three spheres of government; with organs of the civil society (which should include, very importantly, traditional leadership and what we call organs of people's power); as well as business; and last, but not least, members of the community themselves as the captains of their own future – in this way, rural communities will be empowered to be self-reliant and able to take charge of their own destiny.

The Muyexe village that I referred to at the beginning of this address is a pilot site for this programme. Sites in other provinces have already been identified and will be launched in the not-so-distant future, and these include amongst others, in the Northern Cape, North West, Eastern Cape, Free State, Mpumalanga, Western Cape and KwaZulu-Natal.

Small-scale farming, ladies and gentlemen, is a critical component of CRDP delivery in the pilot sites we have referred to above.

Thank you

Dr Joe Phaahla
Deputy Minister, Rural Development and Land Reform

Appendix 3a: Objectives relevant to farmers in Tanzania's policies and strategies

S/No	Policy/ strategy	Issues relevant to small-scale farmers/poor
1	VISION 2025	Ensure food self-sufficiency and food security Absence of abject poverty
2	MKUKUTA	Improve food availability and accessibility at household level in urban and rural areas. Reduce income poverty of both men and women in rural areas
3	ASDP	Achieve a sustained agricultural growth rate of 5 per cent per annum primarily Transform from subsistence to commercial agriculture Strengthen public/private partnerships across all levels of the sector Focus on participatory planning and implementation Reduce proportion of rural food poor (men and women) from 27% in 2000/01 to 14% by 2010. Increase productivity in crop and livestock enterprises by at least 20% Show measurable annual change in % of farmers accessing improved services and infrastructure (by type) Farmers with irrigation: 8% Farmers using ox-ploughs: 18%
4	AMSDP	Increase incomes and food security of the rural poor in Northern and Southern Highlands agro-ecological and marketing zones of Tanzania. Improve structure, conduct and performance of agricultural marketing systems in the country Provide financial incentives to realise the following specific objectives: (i) increased and diversified production of smallholders; and (ii) increased number of medium-scale entrepreneurs who interact with groups of producers and traders in rural areas Agricultural marketing policy development: (i) producer empowerment and market linkages; (ii) financial market support services; and (iii) rural marketing infrastructure development

5	Agricultural Marketing Policy (AMP)	Farmers and agricultural marketing actors to be supported to negotiate and compete effectively in regional and international markets Encourage producers to enter the markets directly instead of using middlemen Promote adherence to quality standards and grade in agricultural products – start with the domestic market Enhance access to agricultural marketing finance Strengthen agricultural marketing extension services
9	Agriculture and Livestock Policy	Increase production growth rates of food crops and livestock products to at least 4% and 5% per annum, respectively Improve standards of living in the rural areas through increased income generation from agricultural and livestock production, processing and marketing Produce and supply raw materials, including industrial crops, livestock, by-products and residues for local industries, while also expanding the role of the sector as a market for industrial outputs through the application of improved production, marketing and processing technologies Develop and introduce new technologies which increase the productivity of labour and land Promote integrated and sustainable use and management of natural resources such as land, soil, water and vegetation in order to conserve the environment Provide support services to the agricultural sector which cannot be provided efficiently by the private sector Promote the access of women and youth to land, credit, education and information Promote agricultural research, extension and training Facilitate the provision of a good infrastructure, especially transport and storage Taxes and subsidies
6	Mini-Tiger Plan	One village, one product programme (OVOP) Scholarship tree planting – I million ha commercial forest project Cash crop SEZ programme GIS application programme for land use and allocation
7	MKURABITA Mpango wa Kurasimisha Rasilimali za Biashara za Wanyonge (Tanzania)	Reduce individual household poverty Improve living standard of the target groups

8	RFSP (rural financial services programme)	Support the design, development and implementation of sustainable rural financial services at the village or ward levels in the form of registered micro-finance institutions (MFIs) Develop a sustainable rural financial network infrastructure Further empower poor rural households to benefit from rural financial services
10	National Land Policy	Access to land, so that all citizens shall have equal and equitable access to land Guarantee women's access to land and security of tenure Protect risk groups such as displaced persons, children and lower-income people
11	Cooperative Development Policy	Eliminate social and economic injustice in the society Transform farmers from subsistence to commercial farmers Enhance farmers' income through processing of produces to obtain added value Provide employment to farmers in off-season periods
12	National Livestock Policy	Contribute towards national food security through increased production, processing and marketing of livestock products Improve standards of living of people engaged in the livestock industry through increased income generation from livestock Increase the quantity and quality of livestock and livestock products as raw materials for local industry and export. Promote the use of draught animal power and biogas utilisation Promote irrigation based on traditional and modern practices and mechanised farming Organise and train farmers in production methods for the full product-cycle Undertake research on production technology and requirements, support through provision of inputs and extension services, and facilitate contractual links with commercial enterprises for the purpose of processing and marketing.

Appendix 3b: Approved and actual expenditures (in TSh billions) for the Ministry of Agriculture, Food Security and Cooperatives

Financial year	Recurrent budget					Development budget			
	Approved budget (a)	Actual expenditure (b)	Variance (a-b)	Variance as % of approved budget (a-b/a)100		Approved budget (c)	Actual expenditure (d)	Variance (c-d/c)	Variance as % of approved budget (c-d/c)100
2000/01	10.3	10.3	0.0	0.0		15.8	3.0	12.8	80.981
2001/02	9.6	8.7	0.9	9.0		16.0	14.7	1.3	8.123
2002/03	16.2	15.7	0.6	3.4		18.6	14.5	4.1	21.88
2003/04	41.5	41.2	0.2	0.6		31.5	19.2	12.3	39.122
2004/05	34.1	0.0	0.0	–		22.4	–	–	–
2005/06	71.4	68.1	3.3	4.6		62.1	29.3	32.8	52.858
2006/07	76.4	58.4	17.9	23.5		45.8	27.8	18.0	39.234
2007/08	71.9	70.0	1.9	2.6		60.1	54.1	6.0	9.918

Source: MAFSC Appropriation Account Books

Appendix 3c: Audit queries in the Ministry of Agriculture Food Security and Cooperatives in Tanzania as per CAG report (June 2008)

- Receipts in cash book but not reflected in bank statements: TShs 129,045,950.
- Purchase of additional assets not accounted for: TShs 1,969,270,000.
- Goods worth TShs 8,971,000 not taken on ledger charges.
- Payment amounting to TShs 36,001,000 without supporting documents.
- Irregular procurement of furniture: TShs 60,375,000.
- Utilisation of TShs 7,435,000 transferred to sub-treasury for seminar and workshop could not be traced.
- Untraced balance of subsidised urea fertilisers: 100 metric tonnes worth TShs 20,500,000.
- Unreceipted subsidised fertiliser to farmers: TShs 30,402,100.
- A main input supplier (name withheld) played the role of stockist for fertiliser worth TShs 91,500,000 contrary to the guidelines issued by Permanent Secretary of MOAFS. He entered into contract with government as main supplier of the subsidised fertilisers for the year 2007/08. The same main supplier was given permits to sell subsidised fertilisers in Ruvuma, but the returns did not show signatures of farmers and price charged.
- 65 tonnes of sulphur dust valued at TShs 35,100,000 were not been delivered to Masasi-Mtwara Cooperative Union (MAMCU) although records provided by Cashew-nut Board of Tanzania (CBT) has shown that such quantities were sold to the agent.
- An amount of TShs 74,448,500 was said to have been allocated to Mkuranga District Council. However, an audit conducted at district council headquarters noted that the officials responsible for distribution and monitoring of agricultural inputs were not aware of how much money was allocated to the district. On the other hand, the records made available to the auditors by the Cashew-nut Board of Tanzania reveal that agricultural inputs worth TShs 74,448,500 were sold to the district.

Source: CAG Report 2008

Appendix 3d: Audit report of the Ministry of Agriculture, Food Security and Cooperatives (million TSh)

Problem	Year					
	2001	2002	2003	2004	2005	2006
Revenue not accounted for					18.7	
Revenue collected but not banked						
Missing revenue receipts books						
Sum questioned revenue	0	0	0	0	18.7	0
Unauthorised expenditure						
Unauthorised expenditure				3.7		
Unvouchered expenditure					9.1	6.5
Improperly vouchered expenditure	39.2	66.9		203.2		4,374.1
Irregular payments	27.2	84.0		8,269.3		110.5
Payments not supported by pro forma invoices						
Sum questioned expenditure	66.392	150.931	198.153	8476.132	226.351	4491.076
Total actual expenditure (supply vote)	10,314.0	8,702.4	15,670.8	41,215.2	35,377.3	68,131.0
Total actual expenditure (develop vote)	13,006.2	14,661.2	14,533.2	19,187.5	22,429.8	29,337.1

Total actual expenditure	23,320.2	23,363.7	30,204.0	60,402.7	57,807.0	97,468.1
Questioned exp. as % of total exp.	0%	1%	1%	14%	0%	5%
General opinion	2	2	2	2	2	3
Supply account	2	2	2	2	0	3
Development account	2	2	2	2	0	3
Deposit account	2	2	2	2	0	3
Revenue account	2	2	2	2	0	3

Key:
No opinion: 0
Adverse: 1
Qualified: 2
Clean: 3

Source: CAG Report 2007

Appendix 3e: Expenditure components by size

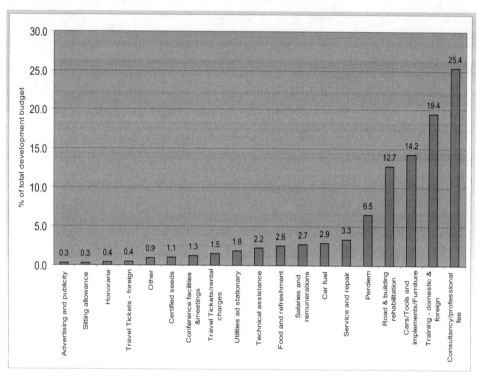

Source: MAFSC, MTEF 2007–2010